HIDDEN ABERDEENSHIRE

The Land

DR FIONA-JANE BROWN

BLACK & WHITE PUBLISHING

First published 2015
by Black & White Publishing Ltd
29 Ocean Drive, Edinburgh EH6 6JL

1 3 5 7 9 10 8 6 4 2 15 16 17 18

ISBN: 978 1 84502 990 6

A CIP catalogue record for this book is available from the British Library.

CREATIVE SCOTLAND
ALBA | CHRUTHACHAIL

Typeset by Creative Link, North Berwick
Printed and bound in Poland
www.hussarbooks.pl

Contents

Introduction

Hidden Aberdeenshire: The Land is the sequel to my previous work, *Hidden Aberdeenshire: The Coast.* I have collected just some of the many stories and legends from landward Aberdeenshire which I found while researching its fascinating past. The country people have always worked hard in order to reap the rewards of the fecund Buchan soil. It would seem, however, that their medieval and Celtic ancestors were far more war-like and brutal than their fisher counterparts, considering the number of battles, murders and Machiavellian intrigues featured. For example, Alexander Stewart, Earl of Mar, was a particularly unpleasant individual who schemed, raped and fought his way to public approval to become the heroic leader of the Lowland army who faced Donald MacDonald, 8th Lord of the Isles, at the Battle of Harlaw. There are more decent 'chiels' like Jamie Fleeman, The Laird of Udny's Feel – whose simple wisdom confounded those with too great a conceit of themselves – and Rev. John Skinner, the minister of Longside, who patiently bore persecution, but could as easily turn on his enemies in verse when the spirit moved him.

From this book you will gain a brief insight into the histories of the men and women who shaped Aberdeenshire for better or worse throughout history. I hope that it will encourage you to delve further for yourselves into the compelling past of this, my home county. To help, I've added a glossary of local words and historic events which may be unfamiliar and a bibliography to set you off on the trail.

As in previous volumes, the stories I have chosen are either entirely new, lesser known or have entirely slipped out of public consciousness. A few are based entirely on oral legends and have never been recorded in print before. I have attempted to restrict my research to Aberdeenshire's historic borders, with only two exceptions: Maryculter's Templar Chapel and Newlands Farm, the latter being the location for the filming of local horror movie, *The Redwood Massacre*. Both sites are in modern Aberdeenshire, but historically are part of Kincardine. I included the tale of the Templar Ghosts because I needed it to contrast with the Scottish Travellers' version attached to the Persephone statue at Pitcaple, and I included the film because some of my friends star in it.

There are tales to interest everyone, whether fans of true crime, historic battles or couthy characters. If I've missed anything out that readers feel should have been included, it was either because I ran out of space, or the locations were not within the historic county borders. As ever, I hope to include them in future volumes.

My books were first inspired by my walking tours, having founded *Hidden Aberdeen Tours* in 2011. For more details, have a look at my website: http://www.hiddenaberdeen.co.uk.

To the landward folk of Aberdeenshire; their history and tongue are rich and deserve to be celebrated by all future generations.

LINN OF DEE TO MARYCULTER

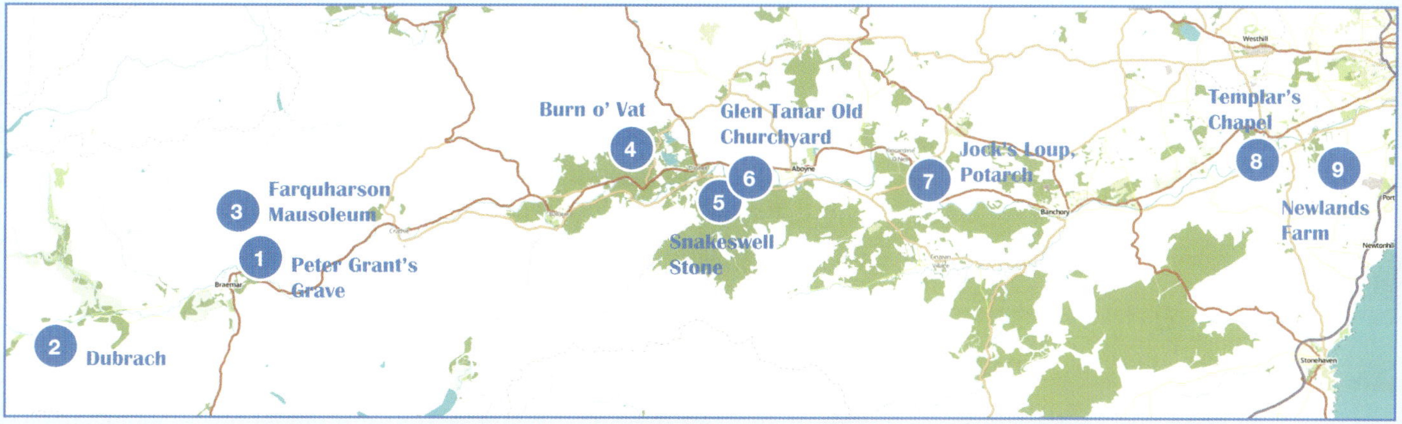
Burn o' Vat
Glen Tanar Old Churchyard
Templar's Chapel
Farquharson Mausoleum
Jock's Loup, Potarch
Newlands Farm
Snakeswell Stone
Peter Grant's Grave
Dubrach
Westhill
Aboyne
Banchory
Braemar
Newtonhill
Stonehaven

1. The Oldest Jacobite – Peter 'Dubrach' Grant's Grave, Braemar Kirkyard

In 1714, the year preceding the first Jacobite Rebellion, Peter Grant was born at the farm toun of Dubrach in Glen Dee. He would espouse Bonnie Prince Charlie's cause in 1745 and be honoured for bravery at the Battle of Prestonpans.

The lonely moor of Culloden where the Jacobite hopes were dashed forever in April 1746 was not dissimilar to Peter's home – a wild, heathery landscape pitted with rocks. As a sergeant major for the Mackintoshes, 'Dubrach', as he was known, was anxious to engage the enemy, roaring, 'Oh, let's throw awa' thae fushionless things o' guns, 'er we get doon upon the smatchets wi' oor swords!' The superior firepower of the Hanoverian army, however, would scatter and decimate the Highland army left to die or be captured by their once beloved prince.

Yet, despite being imprisoned in Carlisle Castle, Dubrach's loyalty to the Stuart cause never wavered in all his long life thereafter; unlike his unfortunate fellows, he was able to escape his prison and return alive to Deeside. Though he had lost his home, he went to live with his son at Westside, Glen Lethnot, and resumed his trade as a tailor, never once betrayed by his neighbours for the price on his head as a Jacobite rebel.

In 1822, two gentlemen travellers on Deeside encountered a man of great age who regaled them with stories of his exploits in the 1745 Jacobite Rebellion and demonstrated to them the use of his broadsword. The travellers were very impressed and also sympathetic to his poverty-stricken state, and so petitioned George IV via Lord Panmure to award a pension to 'Auld Dubrach' as he was now known.

In the summer of that year, legend has it that the old soldier's new friends took him to Edinburgh to meet the king as part of George IV's tartan-clad visit to the Scottish capital. When the monarch met him, he was introduced as 'Peter Grant of Dubrach, your oldest servant', but the latter, after shaking the hand of the Hanoverian king, commented, 'Na, na, yer Majesty, I'm yer auldest enemy!' Evidently George IV took his words in good spirits and awarded him a pension of a pound per week for life.

Auld Dubrach lived until 1824, dying at the age of 110, having even outlived his sixty-five-year-old wife, Mary Cumming. The locals gave the last Jacobite a good send-off, apparently consuming an anker or four gallons of whisky before the internment. Dubrach's good friend, Charles Lamont, had promised to play the pipes at his funeral if he outlived him. 'Old Lamont' was ninety when he played the Jacobite tune 'Wha Widna Fecht For Charlie?' in Braemar graveyard where Peter is buried today next to the Farquharson of Invercauld mausoleum.

2. CSI Dubrach: The Murder of Sgt. Davies – Dubrach Farm Toun, Linn of Dee

There is a more sinister story associated with Dubrach. In 1749, army officer, Sgt. Arthur Davies, who had been billeted at the farm, disappeared, and was later believed to have been murdered. The Englishman was an amiable sort, perhaps too trusting of his host community. While he was quartered at Dubrach with his wife Jean, he would openly wear a silver watch and chain, a silk purse full of gold coins, and two gold rings. Davies often walked alone, usually trying to shoot deer, as he did on the day he disappeared. Despite an extensive search by his men, he was not found.

Soon after, local layabout and reputed poacher, Duncan Clerk, who previously lived with his father in Inverey, was suddenly able to afford the rental of 105 Scots merks on a farm and to marry Elizabeth Downie. The new Mrs Clerk's ring bore an uncanny resemblance to the missing officer's. Speculation grew rife as to Clerk's involvement in Davies' disappearance. It was the discovery of the sergeant's tricorn hat by a servant girl that eventually led to the arrest of Clerk and his supposed partner-in-crime, local forester, Alexander MacDonald.

The trial at Edinburgh's High Court in June 1754 featured the most fantastical evidence from twenty-six-year-old hill shepherd, Alasdair MacPherson, a monoglot Gaelic speaker. The latter testified that he had been woken from his bed by the sergeant's ghost almost a year after Davies had disappeared, commanding him to bury his bones which lay in Glen Christie near Inverey. When asked by defence lawyer in which language the spirit spoke, the shepherd replied, 'In as good Gaelic as ever I heard in Lochaber!' MacPherson found the body, but was too frightened to move it. He was awoken the where the mouldering remains of the sergeant lay. They buried him in the peat and spoke no more of the affair.

Yet there *had* been a witness to the murder – fugitive Jacobite, Angus Cameron. Cameron testified that he saw Clerk and MacDonald standing over a dead deer, when Davies' sudden appearance disturbed them. Clerk dashed forward, striking the sergeant in the chest and MacDonald shot him in the back as he fled.

The outcome of the case caused a sensation when the reputed killers were found 'Not Guilty'; the jury were accused of Jacobite sympathy, protecting their own against the English occupying forces. Yet when the damning evidence came from a ghost and an outlaw, surely it was only sensible to throw it out? To this day, no one has ever revealed the truth about Sgt. Davies' untimely end.

following morning and this time the ghost told him that Clerk and MacDonald were his killers. Seeking help from Duncan Farquharson, whose father now rented Peter Grant's old farm, MacPherson returned to Glen Christie

3. The Black Colonel's Postmortem Movements – Farquharson Mausoleum, Braemar Cemetery

Margaret Farquharson was furious; her husband's newly buried coffin stood inexplicably above the ground, but she knew it was John's way of telling her he wasn't happy. *Curse him and his Annie Bàn, never will I allow them to lie together in death!*

Better known as the Black Colonel for his swarthy complexion and raven hair, John Farquharson of Inverey was a feisty, hot-tempered soldier who had fought alongside 'Bonnie Dundee', aka John Graham of Claverhouse, at the Battle of Killiecrankie in 1689. He had sheltered Dundee at Inverey Castle while they planned their clash with the Government troops loyal to William of Orange, the Protestant replacement for James II, the avowedly Catholic monarch. In 1666, Farquharson was wanted for murder, having slain John Gordon of Brackley in combat. According to

the ballad 'Baron of Brackley', Gordon's widow, Peggy, having long since tired of him, entertained her husband's killer afterwards. Farquharson escaped penalty by remaining in Inverey, an isolated township near Linn of Dee.

Farquharson is also renowned for riding his horse up the narrow gorge at Glen Ey to escape the Redcoats after he had burned Braemar Castle to prevent it being occupied by the enemy force. He hid there, his resting place a rocky shelf later called 'The Colonel's Bed' and watched Inverey Castle being razed to the ground. Apparently his mistress, 'Annie Bàn', meaning fair or blonde-haired Annie, crept up to see him and supplied him with food and drink, much to his second wife Margaret Leith's annoyance. It was Annie's attentions that led John Farquharson to request on his deathbed that he be buried at Inverey in the plot next to hers. Historian Fenton Wyness put it more delicately, writing that Farquharson wanted to be buried 'with his kin'.

Margaret would have deliberately seen to it that this wish was not granted. She probably felt very insecure, being the second wife, and stepmother to John's children, Elizabeth and Peter. Thus the Black Colonel was interred in St Andrew's Cemetery, Braemar. Tradition holds that the day following the funeral, his coffin was found above ground. The gravediggers reburied it, doubtless under Mrs Farquharson's watchful eye. The following day it happened again and a third time, when Margaret finally relented and ordered the coffin to be transported back to Inverey.

All was peaceful until years later, when some rather careless gravediggers struck the Black Colonel's remains. They each stole a tooth from his skull as a souvenir. Stealing from the dead only leads to trouble, as they discovered when Farquharson's ghost visited each in turn, ordering them to return his molars! The terrified men did as they were bid, and the Colonel did not trouble them again. The Farquharson mausoleum still stands in Braemar Cemetery today, but minus John of Inverey's remains.

4. Gilderoy's Hideout – Burn o' Vat, Muir of Dinnet

Howls of laughter pealed around the ancient natural amphitheatre as Patrick 'Gilderoy' MacGregor regaled another tale of villainy to his gang of cattle-rustlers. Yet that hideout, known today as the Burn o' Vat, could not protect them forever; Gilderoy was eventually caught and hanged at Edinburgh's Grassmarket in 1658, aged only thirty-four. It is easy to imagine that this bowl-like cave of stone, created by the action of glacial meltwater full of rocky detritus spinning in a confined space, was the hiding place for one of seventeenth-century Aberdeenshire's most notorious gangs of brigands.

The MacGregor name has always been associated with the more famous Rob Roy. Claiming their descent from Grigor, a prince of Dalriada (Gaelic kingdom based in both Ireland and Argyllshire), the MacGregor clan found themselves in constant conflict with authority. James VI, heavily encouraged by their enemies, the Campbells, proscribed the name MacGregor, effectively outlawing the clan.

Patrick MacGregor hailed from the Howe of Cromar, apparently of a noble family. He was known as 'Gille Ruaidh', the red-haired lad, which English-speakers rendered 'Gilderoy'. According to the *Newgate Calendar*, an English record of executions, Gilderoy wasted his inheritance then killed his mother to gain more money. The account goes on to accuse him of many atrocities, more than likely exaggerated by hearsay and the general hatred of the MacGregor name.

The Marquis of Huntly, George Gordon, apparently trusted Gilderoy to rid Cromar of a local group of thieves, which Gilderoy's gang achieved with ease. However, seeing the riches that these villains had accumulated through cattle-rustling and protection rackets, Gilderoy reckoned it was a quick way of improving his own financial situation. Burn o' Vat, at the foot of Culblean Hill provided an ideal bolt-hole for their schemes.

Gilderoy's most daring raid took place during the wedding of a local man, John Thom, which was attended by all in the district, who therefore left their properties wide open to the MacGregor gang. The incident was recalled in verse:

> Culblean was burnt and Cromar harriet
> An' dowie's the day John Tam wis marriet.

Gilderoy and company stole every beast in the district, destroyed property and generally availed themselves of the Cromar folks' goods. Buoyed up by this success, Gilderoy turned his attentions to the nearby township of Leochel-Cushnie, but the gang fell foul of

the laird, William Forbes of Craigievar, who succeeded in capturing them. Yet again Gilderoy was able to escape prison, supposedly kidnapping and murdering one of the trial judges by stringing him up on the very gallows that would have executed MacGregor. However, Gilderoy's luck finally ran out and he was taken to Edinburgh bound in heavy chains. His 'hanging tree' was built thirty feet high so all could delight in his end. Patrick's old hideout, Burn o' Vat, remains today as a geological curiosity in the Muir of Dinnet Nature reserve.

5. Wilcebe, Man of Many Talents – the Snakeswell Stone, Firmounth Road, Glen Tanar Estate

'The Worm of the Still is the deadliest Snake on the Hill' reads the curious motto inscribed on a granite slab known as the Snakeswell Stone, which sits by an old, leaf-covered well in the Glen Tanar estate. Responsible for this temperance statement and many other intriguing carvings, was Manchester banker, Sir William Cunliffe Brooks, Laird of Glen Tanar (1871–1900). This one-man whirlwind was a Cambridge graduate, MP, benefactor, baronet, father of two, and, according to landscape architect, Thomas Mawson, 'a short-tempered, self-important martinet' redeemed by his many lovable qualities. 'Wilcebe', as he sometimes signed himself, was fond of children; he carried sweeties with him on his travels and cheered many a bairn on a hospital ward.

But Cunliffe Brooks was also a workaholic and responsible for a flurry of building work at Glen Tanar during his lifetime, including estate cottages, the imposing Tower of Ess, the Victory Hall in Aboyne, and Glen Tanar House. Mawson observed that his employer rose at 6am, and sent his piper out to wake the rest of the household at 7am. By this time, Cunliffe Brooks would have already answered all his correspondence and been ready for his regular tour of the estate and supervision of his building projects.

Holidays were no exception; laird and architect risked the wrath of the local minister when they were spotted on a Good Friday by Rev. Nash discussing measurements for the tower at Bridge of Ess. Mawson mentioned that he wouldn't be surprised if they were chastised in the sermon that day. Cunliffe Brooks retorted 'I say he dare not do it, I pay his stipend.' The minister duly denounced them from the platform, resulting in a furious row outside afterwards.

The laird could brook no argument from anyone, especially his tenants. At Ballaterach Farm, where the young Lord Byron spent many summers in a previous generation, Cunliffe Brooks was inspecting building work when the farmer suggested a minor alteration to improve the efficiency of the structure. The laird stormed off in high dudgeon, never to visit the place again.

Despite his dictatorial ways, the aforementioned Snakeswell Stone is just one example of Cunliffe Brooks' eccentric love of all things quirky. Wilcebe's royalist sympathies for his neighbour, Queen Victoria, are obvious; the road around Glen Tanar's mansion was called Queen's Drive, Glen Tanar School features the Diamond Jubilee Fountain, and the Jubilee Stone is situated at Knockie Bridge along with the Queen's Well, dated 1874. He was clearly a moralist too, as the horse-trough inscribed 'Honest water never left Man in the Mire' shows.

Perhaps the strongest indication of how Wilcebe viewed himself, and a testament to his iron-willed determination to create a rural English estate in Deeside, is the motto on the horse-trough at Burnroot Farm off the B976: 'Where there is a Will C.B. There is a Way U.C.'

6. Byron's Mary – Glen Tanar Old Kirkyard

'He widna haud his hands fae ony o' the tools, and he spoiled them completely before he would let them go. My father couldna lay hands on him and he wid take nae tellin'!' Hard to believe that these lines apply to Lord Byron, but at eight years old, he was a typical little terror out of his mother's sight while holidaying in Glen Tanar, supposedly to improve his health.

George Gordon Byron, born in London, but brought up in Aberdeen until the age of ten, was in the awkward position of being poverty-stricken gentry. His absent father, Jack Byron, who died in France in 1791, had spent his mother's fortune and lost them the family seat of Gight Castle. Catherine Gordon attempted to keep decent company with the Robertsons of Ballaterach, the lady of the household reputedly descended from the Lords of the Isles. The woods and mountains appealed greatly to the young boy, who ranged about alone despite his club foot. Though he inadvertently tormented other tenants of the Glen Tanar estate with his fascination with rural life, he was generally liked. With nature also arose young Geordie's first infatuation. The clue appears in his poem 'When I Roved a Young Highlander':

> When I rov'd a young Highlander o'er the dark heath,
> And climb'd thy steep summit, oh Morven of snow!
> . . .
> No feeling, save one, to my bosom was dear;
> Need I say, my sweet Mary, 'twas centred in you?

This 'Mary' had 'ringlets of gold' and blue eyes, leading the Glen Tanar folks to believe he was referring to Mary Robertson, one of the daughters of Ballaterach. Yet in his own diaries, Byron later extoled the virtues of his distant cousin, Mary Duff, a brunette with hazel eyes, whom he visited often in Aberdeen around the same time. The poem continues with Byron's exploration of his romantic feelings inspired by the rugged Deeside landscape:

> Yet it could not be Love, for I knew not the name, –
> What passion can dwell in the heart of a child?
> But, still, I perceive an emotion the same
> As I felt, when a boy, on the crag-cover'd wild

Both Marys were near him in age, and of good families, otherwise, his mother would have kept him out of their way. Yet Byron never consummated his passion with either girl. Both were later married, and when his mother told him of Mary Duff's wedding, his feelings, on his own admission, 'nearly threw [him] into convulsions'. It is not recorded whether he shed tears

for poor Mary Robertson, whose husband died soon after her marriage. She lived a widow in the city until 1867, outliving her childhood admirer by forty-three years. Mary is buried in Glen Tanar's old kirkyard with her parents and remembered fondly as 'Byron's Mary' whatever the real truth might have been.

7. The Great Escape – Jock Young's Loup, Potarch, Deeside

Rich travellers on Deeside in the later decades of the seventeenth century often ran the risk of highway robbery. There was no gang more celebrated than the sons of James 'Caird' Young. The eldest, Peter, built a fearsome reputation as the Houdini of his day, able to escape any prison in the country.

Peter's youngest brother, John or Jock Young, although perhaps not as skilled in prison-breaking, certainly shared Peter's bravado. Jock had been imprisoned at Aboyne and was being taken to Aberdeen for trial on a charge of illegal whisky distilling. He broke free of his guards near Potarch and dashed down to the riverbank. It is very likely he and his brothers had fished in the Dee for salmon, caring nothing for licences or landowners, thus Jock would have known where the rocks in the river formed a crossing, albeit with a large gap in between.

In those days the only way for the ordinary public to cross the Dee was by ferry, the Telford-designed bridge not being constructed until 1813. There was a legendary kelpie or water-horse, which often terrorised the ferryman and his customers by leaping onto the boat after dark and threatening to drown them all. Jock had no fear of such entities, especially in daylight. He careered down into the shallows, perhaps with his wrists still manacled, and made the jump to the rocks at the far side, leaving his pursuers screaming their threats after him.

Yet was this the same Jock Young who, years later, would quail before the face of the civic executioner, Robbie Welsh, after his celebrated brother had finally been brought to justice and hanged at Aberdeen?

Jock's gang, which included some of his cousins, were hiding out at Chapel of Garioch when a furious row began. Jock stabbed his cousin Hugh Graham several times until he was lying dead at Jock's feet. Horrified at having killed his kinsman, he fled.

The murder was reported and Jock soon arrested, tried and sentenced to death. He was to be hanged on 11 December 1801 on the gallows in Castlegate, an attempt by his allies to free him having failed. Jock walked onto the scaffold, wrists bound behind him, accompanied by a local priest who had sat up with him the night before the execution. He saw Welsh, grinning like a skull, holding the white shroud to dress him for his death. Whether it was the executioner's malicious smile, or the thought that his body would be sent for dissection afterwards, Jock exclaimed 'I dinna like tae hae that creature Robbie Welsh's hands aboot me!' The kindly priest intervened and lifted the shroud over Jock's head.

Yet it is for his extraordinary leap at Potarch that he is remembered; the half-submerged line of rocks is still known as 'Jock Young's Loup'.

8. Ghosts of Templar Park – Templar Chapel, Maryculter House Hotel

Within the grounds of Maryculter House Hotel lie the ruins of an ancient chapel associated with the Knights Templar since AD 1225. A fabulous legend has been woven here to explain the sighting of two ghosts – a knight in full armour on horseback and a woman clad in black often seen in Templars' Park.

Godfrey Wedderburn hailed from Maryculter and was inspired to join the Templar Order, espousing its vows of chastity and poverty. After one of many battles against the Saracen or Muslim forces in the Holy Lands, Godfrey was left unconscious on the battlefield, terribly wounded. He woke later to find himself in a cave with a beautiful young woman attending to his injuries. It was apparent from her dress and dusky skin that she was of the very race he and his fellow knights were intent on killing.

Days passed and the pair fell in love, but not once did Godfrey ever betray the vows of his order, keeping silent to the maiden of his feelings. On the day he finally had to leave, the maiden gave him a magical golden necklet, which, she explained, would protect him from harm as long as he remained pure of heart.

Back home in Maryculter, months later, attending Mass at the Templars' Chapel, Godfrey was astonished when his Saracen maiden, her clothes dusty from her epic journey, entered and flung her arms around him, declaring her love. The Master of the Order was furious that a woman should enter their sacred space, especially a Saracen, and ordered her to be removed. Godfrey pleaded with the Master, telling him of their meeting and her kindness, but he in turn accused the knight of sexual misconduct. Godfrey's temper

flared and he struck the Master to the ground. Such disobedience was punishable by death.

While the poor maiden was being cared for in the infirmary, she was unaware her beloved was being taken to a lonely spot by the Dee to be executed. The moment the fatal weapon struck Godfrey in the heart, the maiden's scream echoed all around them. She was suddenly there, howling in Arabic that they were both innocent. Pulling the golden ring from Godfrey's neck, she dared the Master to wear it to test the veracity of his opinion. Descrying her superstitious charm, he boldly placed it around his neck. His words of derision soon turned to a scream of horror as a single bolt of lightning struck him, obliterating his entire being. The maiden cried out triumphantly, seized the executioner's knife and plunged it into her own heart. The knight and the maiden were finally reunited in death. The Saracen charm was lost, but if found, it is said to protect the wearer from physical harm . . . only if they are pure in heart, unlike Maryculter's judgemental Templar Master.

9. It Looks Different in the Movies – Newlands Farm, Hill of Blairs, Maryculter

Local film director David Ryan Keith could not have chosen a better location for his chilling slasher horror flick, *The Redwood Massacre*, than the farmstead of Newlands. It stands between two of Deeside's ancient trackways, the Causey Mounth and Elsick Mounth. Artefacts of the ancient past are to be found all along these routes. Elsick hosts the Roman marching camps of Normandykes and Raedykes, as well as the 'Lang Stane', marked with Celtic Ogham script perhaps indicating the burial site of a local seer. The Causey, or Cowie, Mounth was the only coastal track from Stonehaven to Aberdeen, terminating at the Brig of Dee, used by the Marquis of Montrose's forces when they arrived to battle Lord Burleigh's Presbyterian army at Justice Mills in 1644.

David's locally cast film tells the gruesome tale of a group of friends who decide to camp near a farmhouse where the farmer hacked his wife and daughter to death with an axe before killing himself. One of the girls reveals that the only witness was the farmer's son, who supposedly went mad and disappeared. One by one, our group of clean-cut teens end up at the mercy of a ruthless axe-wielding psychopath whose face is hidden by a sack mask. Gallons of stage blood spatter the screen from the beginning as the axe-man slays a couple in the woods near the farm; one is a rather annoying rascal played by Aberdeen actor Alec Westwood. The latter is better known for his portrayal of Folly the Jester in the 1990s children's programme *Knightmare*.

David describes the slasher genre as 'one of the most popular and cheapest to film'. Using Scottish

scenery was a deliberate decision to interest American audiences, as he explained: ‘From the feedback we’re getting, they find it refreshing having a film like this set in an unfamiliar location.’ Filming took six months, mainly in winter, with copious amounts of ‘sauce’ soaking the cast at every opportunity. Actress Lisa Cameron, who plays the sensible Pamela, commented, ‘There was so much blood! . . . I had to spend most of the shoot drenched in almost *Carrie*-amounts of blood, outdoors in winter in the Northeast of Scotland! The novelty can wear off!’

Newlands Farm, ten minutes south of Maryculter, is situated near the curiously named Clochandighter Wood. Consisting of a farmhouse and three large barns which play host to the killer’s lair in the film, Newlands appears on maps as early as 1843, part of the Maryculter estate, with neighbouring farms including Greenloaning and Auchintoul. Dominating the area is the seventeenth-century mansion house of Auchlunies. With its imposing architecture and eerie Victorian farm touns, the area, correctly known as Hill of Blairs, really is the perfect setting for David’s blood-soaked fantasy.

DYCE TO AIKEY BRAE

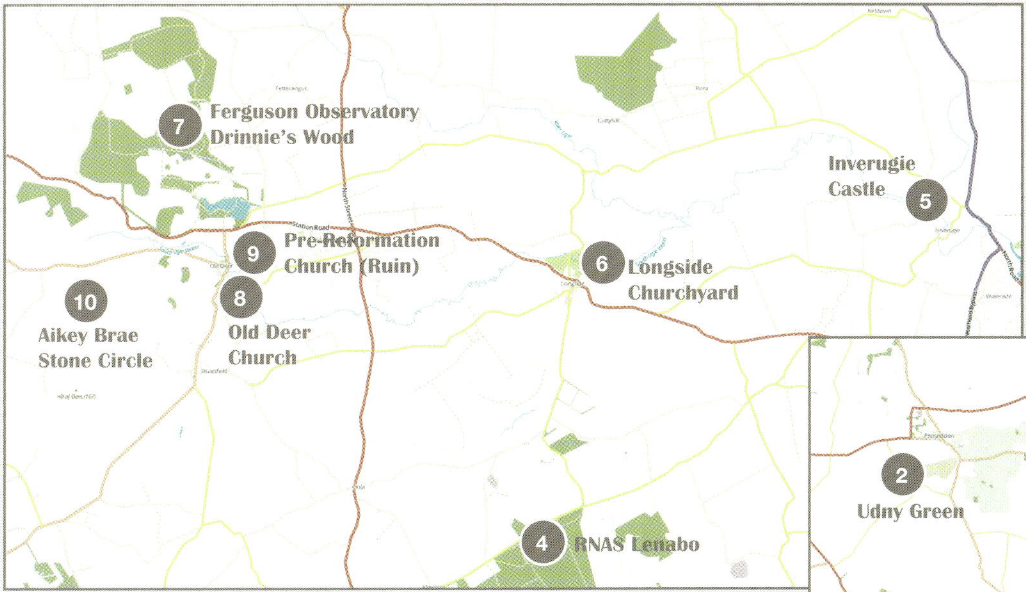
Ferguson Observatory
Drinnie's Wood
7
Inverugie
Castle
5
9
Pre-Reformation
Church (Ruin)
6
Longside
Churchyard
10
8
Aikey Brae
Stone Circle
Old Deer
Church
4
RNAS Lenabo
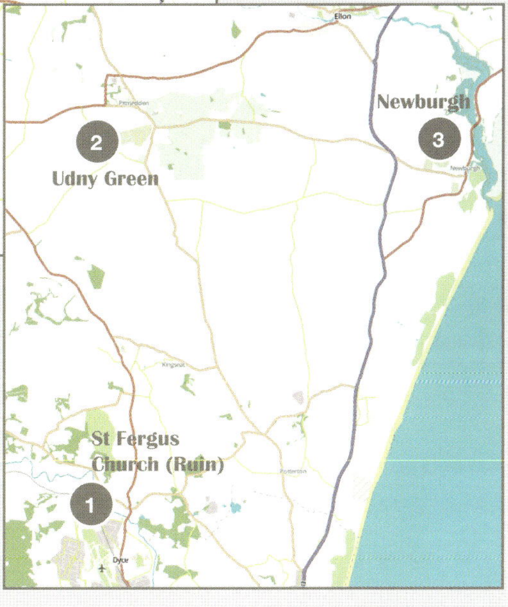
Newburgh
3
2
Udny Green
St Fergus
Church (Ruin)
1

1. What Happened to the Luftwaffe? – St Fergus Kirkyard, Dyce

While the RAF defended the English coast at Portland in thick fog on 12 July 1940, the shipyard workers at Hall, Russell & Company in Fittie, Aberdeen, were thinking about their lunchtime sandwiches. Those who would leave the premises to buy a snack from one of the numerous local shops would stand in horror a few moments later as their colleagues disappeared under the carnage of a huge bomb blast. The German Heinkels responsible for the bombing in broad daylight were soon pursued by members of 603 Squadron from Dyce, scrambled just after the raid. The sky over the Torry Battery was soon the setting for a dramatic dogfight which resulted in one enemy aircraft being hit. The pilot was twenty-four-year-old August Skokan, who somehow steered his stricken plane across the Dee towards the foot of Anderson Drive. The wing tip caught a tree and the Heinkel 111 crashed in flames into the ice rink, which was under construction nearby, killing Skokan and his three colleagues.

Locals remember the dramatic suddenness of the air raid and the plane crash and the scramble for souvenirs afterwards at the Brig of Dee by young lads. One of the latter, Bob Gibb, who was ten years old at the time, had already seen the horrible aftermath in Fittie's York Street which had included the old Neptune Bar, the second storey of which had collapsed onto the lunchtime drinkers. Bob and his cousin Walter reached the Brig of Dee by tram and dashed up to the wreck. Bob later remembered: 'One of the crew had obviously tried to bail out and met his death trapped in the bomber's half-open door. The police were everywhere, but we managed to

sneak past in a search for souvenirs.' Bob's treasures included 'a number of cartridge cases, a couple of pieces of parachute harness, and a small piece of the wreckage'. The remains of the plane were later displayed in the quad at Marischal College while the German airmen were given a proper military funeral and interred at the old Dyce cemetery overlooking the River Don.

The four fliers are still buried in the shadow of the medieval ruin of St Fergus Chapel, Dyce, today, unlike many other foreign nationals whose remains were repatriated after the war. Paul Plischke was twenty-five, Herbert Huck twenty-one, and their youngest colleague, Georg Kerkhoff was only three days short of his twenty-first birthday when their plane crashed. There are six other Luftwaffe personnel interred at the cemetery: four who died in a plane crash off Cruden Bay in 1941, and two shot down over Peterhead a few days before the raid at Hall, Russell & Company. Alongside them are the RAF personnel, the majority also in their early twenties. Silence reigns where once these men presided over death and destruction.

2. Beating the Bodysnatchers – Mort House, Udny Green Kirkyard

The practice of anatomy before 1832 suffered from a shortage of cadavers on which to practise. In north-east Scotland, rather than 'professional' resurrectionists, our graveyards were plagued by the medical students themselves who would attempt to dig up and steal freshly buried corpses for their studies. After the scandalous trial of serial killers Burke and Hare in 1829, who murdered to order for Dr Robert Knox of Edinburgh, people feared for their lives, convinced there was a 'burker' around every dark corner. The Travelling community felt especially at risk from the 'Noddies', as they called the medical students, a term for the spritely, two-wheeled horse-gig often employed on nightly grave-robbing excursions. Their itinerant lifestyle meant that no one would miss them should they fall foul of resurrectionists. Maggie Stewart told of how her father and grandparents escaped with their lives when the 'burkers' coach' came hunting for them when they stayed at a particular farm, despite the farmer warning them to go elsewhere. Maggie's grandfather had to stab the dog belonging to the medics to prevent it barking and giving away their hiding place.

In country kirkyards, folk invented various methods of protecting their dead, including setting gin-traps, building mortsafes, watch-houses and mort houses. Many of the latter are found in Aberdeenshire including those at Culsalmond, Hatton of Fintray and Belhelvie, but the most original is the mort house at Udny Green. Designed as a secure vault in which to temporarily place bodies until they had decomposed to the extent that they were worthless to the anatomists, the mort house was built in the kirkyard. By 1832, the canny villagers of Udny Green decided rather than a watch-house, they would fool the 'burkers' in a far more ingenious manner after accepting the proposed design from John Marr of Cairnbrogie. This mort house was built by Alexander Wallace, a mason from Smiddyhill, and Thomas Smith, a wright from Oldmeldrum, as a double-skinned circular structure of solid, rough-hewn granite with a conical slate roof. It was secured by exterior oak and interior iron doors. Inside, Smith installed a raised wooden rotating platform on which coffins would be placed until they had completed a full circuit and were then removed for burial. The entire project cost £114, approximately £10,000 in modern money.

The mort house was maintained by subscription. Strict rules governed its use, including stipulations for the construction of coffins, which had to be 'of well-seasoned fir 7/8 inches thick and completely air-tight, or if the deceased had been suffering an infectious condition, the body had to be encased in tin or lead.' By the time the mort house was complete, the Anatomy Act 1832, which regulated the supply of cadavers to the medical profession, rendered it obsolete. Now it stands as a curiosity in the corner of the village kirkyard, locked for good, empty of coffins containing mouldering corpses.

3. Jamie Fleeman and the Great Iron Chest – Knockhall Castle, Newburgh

James Fleming, better known as Jamie Fleeman, the 'Laird o' Udny's Feel', could be described as the last professional 'court jester' in Scotland. Born in 1713 near Longside, he is described thus by local historian, James Pratt:

> His countenance, indescribably or even painfully striking, wore that expression which at once betrays the absence of sound judgement. His head large and round – his hair . . . rendered by constant exposure to the weather, a dingy fox-colour, and not sleek, but standing on end, as if poor Jamie had been frightened out of his wits – indicated that his foolishness was not assumed but real.

Yet it was Jamie's razor-sharp wit that endeared him to many, including his first employer, Alexander Guthrie of Ludquharn, who gave him a glowing reference when he moved to John, the Laird of Udny's household.

Jamie had many noble friends, including the Countess of Erroll, an avowed Jacobite, who often employed him to carry messages to fellow supporters of the Stuart cause. Yet it was the Udnys to whom he demonstrated greatest loyalty. The Udnys had been in the area since David II granted a charter confirming their lands to ancestor, Ronald of Uldney in the fourteenth century. John Udny purchased Knockhall Castle from Lord John Sinclair in 1633. Udny Castle, the family seat, was at this time in the possession of William Seaton who had married Lord Udny's daughter and heiress, Helen.

In 1734, Jamie Fleeman was in his bedroom at Knockhall, practising his chanter when one of the family dogs came in and pulled at his shirt. Being a great lover of canines, he opened the door, presuming it wanted to go outside, but his keen senses smelt smoke, and Jamie quickly discovered the castle to be on fire. He raised the alarm with the laird's gardener, a good friend of his, then dashed to the charter room where the family's important documents were kept in a huge iron chest. The latter, which normally took three men to lift, was hefted up and out of the window by Jamie, thus saving the contents. The laird's feel raced outside and skipped about, delighted with his achievement. Yet he was also rejoicing for another reason; his old nemesis, the Udny's housekeeper, was still abed and unaware she was in danger of her life. The gardener pleaded with Jamie to rouse her, which he eventually did, declaring to the cantankerous old lady, 'Lucky, lucky, rise or ye'll get het hurdies or lang!' For his pains, Jamie received a life pension of sixpence and a peck of meal per week. The 'fool' was not perhaps as foolish as observers actually believed. Jamie's deathbed plea 'dinna bury me like a beast' in 1778 was answered by a Christian burial in Longside kirkyard where his memorial remains today.

4. A Lost Relic of the Great War – RNAS Lenabo

From a bog in the middle of nowhere rose the Lenabo 'Soos'. The dialect word for sows or female pigs was an appropriate nickname for the giant rubber-clad airships which would hover over the coast during the Great War. In 1915, RNAS *Longside* was created to house these blimps, which would patrol the north-east coast for enemy submarines. An army of naval personnel battled the muddy terrain and a Buchan winter to build hangars, gasworks, engineering shops, canteens, accommodation and a track spur from the Formartine and Buchan Railway. Manson 4-4-0 locomotives pulled trucks of equipment to the site from Peterhead railway station as construction continued apace. A sister station, Auldbar Road, near Montrose was set up for the refuelling of airships flying south of Aberdeen.

Oxonian William L. Morgan who was stationed at Lenabo, remembers the 'silver sausages' with affection. Having been part of the advance team, he worked on demolishing Bogend croft, which had stood on the site. William described Lenabo as looking like a 'primeval swamp', when he encountered the 'timber cabins, lit with oil lamps, and equipped with earth closets . . . It took months of unremitting toil by Royal Navy artisans and an outside contractor (Tawse of Aberdeen) before adequate buildings were erected and services laid on.'

The Soos were difficult to handle in the prevailing winds, making the task of patrolling inshore waters nigh impossible on stormy days. One Soo almost came to grief at Peterhead's Smith Embankment in 1917 when the motor failed and the fabric of the airship was torn after sailing too close to the Town House weathervane. Fortunately, crowds of spectators ran forward and clutched the trailing guy ropes, holding the airship as it bumped down at the edge of the South Bay.

The 'Gasbaggers', as the navy men were known, seemed to spend more time entertaining themselves and the locals. Lenabo boasted a cinema, usually for newsreels, a church for Sabbath devotions and a number of shops. There was a theatre troupe called The Gasbags, who regularly performed shows attended by naval personnel and inhabitants of the neighbouring farms. Their production *Hello Longside* featured a fourteen-piece orchestra aided by locals, George Duncan and John May of Peterhead. There was even a station magazine *The Battlebag,* which was printed by P. Scrogie, Peterhead's long-established press. Alongside accounts of the tragedy of airship C25, downed in the North Sea after a U-Boat encounter, were editorials concerning the sporting feats of the station crew, including a football match where Aberdeen's 3rd Gordon Highlanders beat

RNAS Lenabo 4–1. But, as the war came to a close, the RAF took over from the navy and Lenabo became surplus to requirements. By 1920, the airship station was no more, sold eventually to the Forestry Commission for £5,000, leaving the Lenabo Soo to fly into history.

5. The Castle at the Bottom of the Garden – Inverugie

Retired doctor Alexander Thain has a castle at the bottom of his garden. When he purchased the Castle Coachhouse of Inverugie, the ruins of the medieval seat of the Keiths lay next door.

Inverugie estate originally belonged to Sir Reginald le Cheyne. Sadly he had no male heirs, thus Marion Cheyne brought the estate into the Keith family when she married her second husband, Sir John Keith. John's father Edward Keith was Great Marischal of Scotland, a title conferred on their ancestor, Hervey de Keth by William the Lion. When John's descendant, William Keith, 5th of Inverugie died in 1521, he left two daughters; the eldest, Margaret, married her cousin, William Keith, 3rd Earl Marischal, around 1538. Inverugie thus became the home of the Earls Marischal.

Architectural historians believe that the original 'Cheyne's Tower' was of the motte-and-bailey variety (i.e. a wooden keep built on a mound with a lower courtyard). From Dr Thain's kitchen window, the view over the river suggests that the keep was sited where the coach house is now. Inverugie was thought to have been built of stone from the time of Margaret Keith's marriage to Earl Marischal William. There is an engraved plaque over an archway leading into a courtyard bearing the date 1670.

The most famous resident was George Keith, the 5th Earl Marischal, who succeeded his uncle William. In 1595, George founded Marischal College on the site of the old Greyfriars' or Franciscan monastery as a Protestant rival to Kings College in Old Aberdeen. George's relative by marriage, James VI, gave royal ascent to the university's foundation, making it the first not to have been endorsed by the Pope.

George Keith, 10th Earl Marischal lost Inverugie and his other lands when he and his brother James were accused of treason for supporting the Jacobite Rebellion in 1715. Though the pair fled to Europe, George would eventually return once more, only to see his beloved home in ruins. He wept and begged his coachman to take him away, never to look upon Inverugie again. Many centuries before, Scotland's most famous bad-tempered prophet, Thomas the Rhymer, had made a gloomy prediction over a large boulder in a field near Inverugie:

> As lang's this stane stands on this craft
> The name o Keith shall be alaft
> But when this stane begins to fa'
> The name o' Keith shall wear awa'

The stone was removed in 1763 to be used in the building of St Fergus Church. Four years later, the Keiths' final possession, their Aberdeen town house, was demolished to make way for Marischal Street. The castle's present guardian, Dr Thain, is always happy to show it to interested visitors, ensuring that the Keith name will never fully wear away despite the Rhymer's curse.

6. Tullochgorum – Rev. John Skinner's Gravestone, Longside Kirkyard, Longside

Scots churchmen throughout history seem to have been endowed with great literary ability, and Rev. John Skinner, born in Birse but later the Episcopal minister of Longside, was no exception. He could write in Scots, English and Latin with equal skill. Yet the verses for which Skinner was remembered were those of 'The Reel of Tullochgorum', which no less than Robert Burns described as 'the best Scots sang I ever saw'.

Rev. Skinner, though brought up in a Presbyterian household, joined the Episcopal Church in the late 1730s. This was no small decision, as it cost him his schoolmaster's job. He had to move to Shetland securing the post of private tutor to the Sinclair family. Happily it was also where John met his wife, Grissel Hunter. By the time their first son was born in 1742, the Skinners had returned to the mainland and John had been ordained at Longside.

These were dangerous times, however, as government troops attacked all Episcopal churches and manses, believing the whole denomination to be on the side of Bonnie Prince Charlie. Skinner himself was no enemy of the Protestant Hanoverian monarchy, yet this meant nothing to rapacious soldiers intent on destruction. In July 1746, following Culloden, a local informer brought the Redcoats to Longside; it was said she was seen exulting as Skinner's church was razed to the ground.

With no church, the minister preached from the manse to small groups of his congregation sitting in different rooms or standing in the garden, all to evade the legal restrictions against Episcopal services. In 1753, again due to this particular female informer, Rev.

Skinner found himself imprisoned for six months at Old Aberdeen's tiny prison. It is little surprise considering he wrote scurrilous verses against his persecutor, describing her as a 'shrine-destroying Jezebel', after the pagan queen of Israel. In 1760, things began to improve; George III was far more tolerant of the Scottish Episcopalians, leaving Skinner to continue his ministry in peace.

'Tullochgorum', which contains the lines 'Let Whig and Tory all agree', represents John Skinner's amazing capacity for tolerance, but also his wit against the proud and foolish. The composition originated after a hot debate at the house of his friend, Mrs Montgomery in Ellon, who, exasperated with her guests, begged Skinner to write words to what was a popular fiddle tune. She is immortalised in the opening stanza:

> Come gie's a sang, Montgomery cried
> And lay your disputes all aside.

Skinner makes clear his distaste for those who would be 'oppression's tool', and declares:

> May envy gnaw his rotten soul
> And discontent devour him.

He lived to see his church freed from persecution, yet experienced the sorrow of outliving his beloved Grissel, who died aged eighty. Eighty-six-year-old John died peacefully on 16 June 1807 in Aberdeen, surrounded by his family.

7. The Admiral's Folly – Ferguson Observatory, Drinnie's Wood, Fetterangus

'Splendid, splendid!' called the eminent naval gentleman, applauding as he observed his own horse romp to victory once again at the Pitfour Estate racing circuit. In 1845, at the age of fifty-seven, 'The Admiral', as he was remembered, built an observatory for the dual purpose of viewing his horseracing track and surveying his lands. George Ferguson, who would not reach the rank of admiral until he was actually seventy-two, was the fifth Laird of Pitfour. His father, George Senior, had not spent much time in Aberdeenshire owing to his position as Governor of Trinidad and Tobago. But young George, having been in the navy since the age of seventeen, would spend a vast amount of the family's fortune on entertainments and follies at Pitfour. Folk often say 'like father, like son', and perhaps it was true of the two George Fergusons, who were the opposite of their financially prudent forebears. Governor George's brother, Patrick Ferguson – inventor of the breech-loading rifle – described him as 'the little man monster' when he was a child, having been spoilt on account of ill health. The fifth laird enjoyed his time at sea, fighting against the French in both Revolutionary and Napoleonic Wars. But, when he inherited his title in 1821, George was like the typical sailor on shore leave; he spent money like it was going out of fashion and partied as only the rich could.

The observatory, constructed of local brick with a white harled exterior, was erected in Drinnie's Wood, measuring fifty feet in height, designed by Aberdeen architect John Smith. Inside was a wooden spiral staircase leading to the viewing floor; a modern metal

staircase had to be installed when the council restored the building in 1993. The wood itself was almost 400 feet above sea level, providing a perfect sight line over George's racecourse. The latter was laid out near White Cow Woods; a flat four-and-a-half-mile circular course which passed through the farmlands of Auchrynie, Cabra and Gaval before turning back onto the final straight at Cairnorchies. Though nicknamed 'The Ascot of the North', it was a practice course for George's jockeys to perfect their skills to ride at the likes of the Musselburgh and Perth Races.

Though Admiral George may have appeared a feckless character, he had lost his first wife Elizabeth Holcombe when she died giving birth to their first child in 1814. He ran from his grief by going back to the navy. It was not until 1825, after succeeding to the estate, that he remarried, ironically enough into a family with naval connections. His wife Elizabeth Jane Rowley was the niece of Arthur Wellesley, the Duke of Wellington, with whom George would have been well acquainted. Admiral Ferguson died aged seventy-six in London, succeeded by his son, George, the sixth and final Laird of Pitfour.

8. This Splendid Little Book – Site of Deer Monastery, Old Deer

'May it be on the conscience of everyone with whom this splendid little book shall be that he should give his blessing on the soul of the poor wretchling who wrote it.' So runs the colophon at the end of the gospel manuscript known as *The Book of Deer*. The plaque on the wall of Old Deer Parish Church today tells us that it was written 'in the Celtic monastery in this vicinity . . . which includes the oldest known examples of Scottish Gaelic.'

Sixteenth-century geographer Robert Gordon of Straloch recorded that this monastery was situated 'in a low-lying valley wholly covered with wood in bygone days', very likely the land just behind the present parish church, stretching into the estate of Aden. This monastery was in existence from around the late sixth century until the foundation of the Cistercian one in AD 1214. Deer and its book were completely forgotten until Cambridge University librarian Henry Bradshaw came upon the manuscript in 1860, sharing his discovery with historian friends who went on to publicise his discovery throughout the academic community.

The Book of Deer itself is a ninth-century 'pocket gospel', a small manuscript written on parchment and carried around in a leather satchel, suggesting the monks used it as they went out in the countryside to preach to the local Pictish population. What really had excited Bradshaw were the notes that had been written into the margins and on empty folios. These told the story of Deer's foundation and recorded the land grants from local chieftains over the previous two centuries. Why had they done so? The final addition to the manuscript reveals the truth – a confirmation

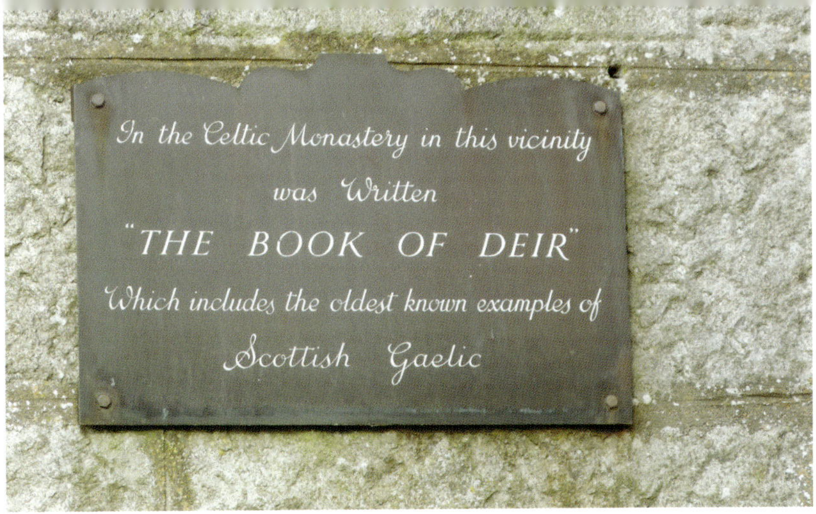

grant from King David I of Scots himself, stating 'the clergy of Deer are to be quit and immune from all lay service and exaction', i.e. from paying any rent or taxes on their lands. It seems the Picts of the East expected both church and lay person to pay their dues, not something the Celtic church was used to, so royal protection was sought by presenting written proof of the land grants which had been given freely in previous generations.

Antiquarian John Stuart, writing in 1869, described the language of the notes as 'the vernacular Gaelic of Alba', penned in the eleventh and twelfth centuries. By this time, the old Pictish tongue would have been superseded by the Q-Celtic Irish of the West, and the monks were local men, writing as they spoke. It would be another three centuries before Gaelic would appear in print, thus this really was and still is a gem of linguistic history, as well as a snapshot of late Celtic and early medieval Buchan. Today, modern technology has allowed the *Book of Deer* to be digitised and it is available to all via Cambridge University's website.

9. Protest at the Kirk!: The Rabbling of Deer – Pre-Reformation Church, Old Deer

Beloved Episcopalian priest George Keith had not been dead a year when a furious riot broke out at his old kirk of Deer in March 1711. His former parishioners had no desire to welcome their new incumbent, John Gordon, and his Presbyterian ways. For the folk of the north east, the Scottish Episcopal Church represented the closest links with the old Roman faith, condemned since the Reformation, and supported the royal house of Stuart, rather than the imposed house of Hanover. The Covenanters' Wars and persecution of Royalists did little to sway the locals to accept this new form of church government. John Gordon's appointment stirred up the parishioners of Deer to such an extent they decided to fight for possession of their church. This was the medieval original, the ruins of which still stand today behind the present kirk, built in 1788.

The university-educated minister was also the son of Aberdeen's then provost, thus he had powerful friends on whom to call. Rev. Gordon's father rode with him from Aberdeen at the head of an armed force from the Castlegate Barracks out to his new church, expecting trouble. When they reached the kirk, there was no one in sight, but the gate was locked and barricaded with large granite boulders. The local magistrate ordered the troop of soldiers and constables to force open the gate, followed by Rev. Gordon and members of the presbytery. The old kirk was accessed by a narrow close between the houses, and the minute the men advanced, they found themselves pelted with a barrage of missiles, thrown by the congregation who had been hiding on the rooftops. The militia was ordered to fire their muskets

parishioners hooting and shouting, as well as drinking 'the Pretender's health in the streets'. The company made quite clear their support for the exiled James Francis Stuart, son of the deposed James II.

However, the law was on the side of the Presbyterians; the rioters were warned by Lord Grange, Justice Clerk, who arbitrated between the parties, that Rev. Gordon should be allowed peaceable access to the kirk and be accepted as their minister. Those involved in the protest, later known as the 'Rabbling of Deer', were fined for damages. Yet there was still hope for the Episcopalians when Parliament

into the sky to deter their attackers, but to no avail. A furious brawl broke out in the lane, the new minister unable to even gain a foothold in his new charge. The presbytery pulled Rev. Gordon away to complete their ordination ceremony elsewhere, leaving the victorious

took up their cause, passing the 1712 Toleration Act, which allowed them to worship in the Anglican manner without interference from other bodies. Today St. Drostan's Episcopal and Old Deer Parish Churches stand across from each other, neighbours and friends.

10. The Battle of Aikey Brae – Parkhouse Hill, Aikey Brae, Old Deer

In the millennia since its construction, Aikey Brae's prehistoric stone circle has witnessed many events, but none worse than a heinous act of slaughter in 1308. Aikey Brae, just outside Old Deer, is better known for its traditional horse fair, but in 1996, Stuartfield man Billy Rennie reckoned he had located the site of a bloody conflict on the slopes of Parkhouse Hill. The Battle of Aikey Brae was a skirmish involving the dispersing forces of John Comyn, Earl of Buchan, and the royal army of Robert the Bruce, who put the former to flight after the Battle of Barra near Inverurie in May 1308. Billy had discovered by a quick dig of a spade that twelve inches down, the earth was charred black as if burned by fire. This, Billy believed, was hard evidence of Bruce's campaign of vengeance against the Comyns known as 'The Herschip of Buchan', a phrase coined by John Barbour in his fourteenth-century epic poem, *The Brus*. Barbour describes how Bruce 'had his men burn all Buchan from end to end, sparing none.' The devastation was such that 'for fifty years, men bewailed the Herschip of Buchan.'

In 1845 the minister of New Deer wrote that Bruce had 'gone in pursuit of the Cummins to . . . Aikey Brae. In memory of this victory, the market of Aikey fair is said to have been established on the spot where the battle was fought.' Although the tale dropped out of local consciousness, the Travelling folk still carried it with them, the area being a popular campsite for them. As late as 1952, Jimmy MacBeath, a Scottish Traveller from Portsoy, Banffshire, was recorded by folklorist Hamish Henderson relating the story of Aikey Brae's gory past:

then, and he cried oot efter he had killed the Comyns, 'Behold, I have slain the Comyns!' Of course, it wis efter that, Aikey Fair wis founded.

Such a story was far removed from the legend I had been taught at primary school of the packman named Aikey who fell into Ugie Water and then laid out all his goods on Parkhouse Hill to dry. He soon found that the monks from nearby Deer Abbey were impressed by his newly dried wares and bought the lot, prompting him to return the following year and establish a market and horse fair on the same site. The enjoyment of Aikey Fair probably had a hand in wiping away the terrible memory of Bruce's acts of brutality, but now the fair is gone, the king's crime has resurfaced to be remembered anew by the present inhabitants of Buchan.

Tae let ye understand, it wisna much o' a battle; the Comyns tried t' overpower the Bruces . . . so fan the Comyns came doon there, there wis a pitched battle . . . The Bruce, he got strong

KINTORE TO INVERYTHAN

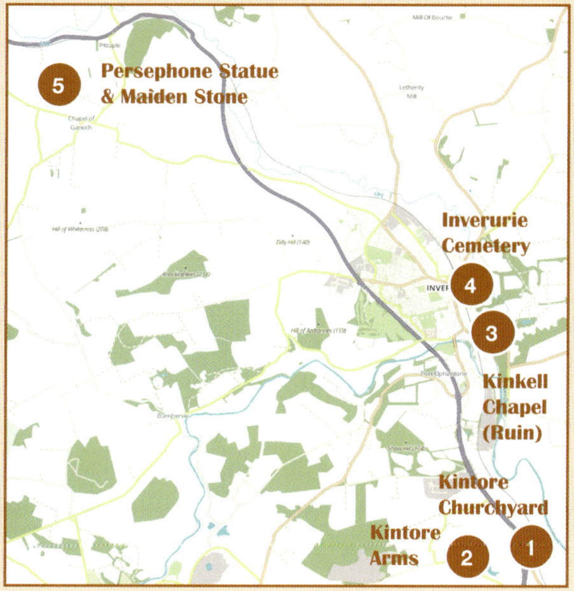
5 Persephone Statue & Maiden Stone
Inverurie Cemetery
4
3
Kinkell Chapel (Ruin)
Kintore Churchyard
Kintore Arms
2
1

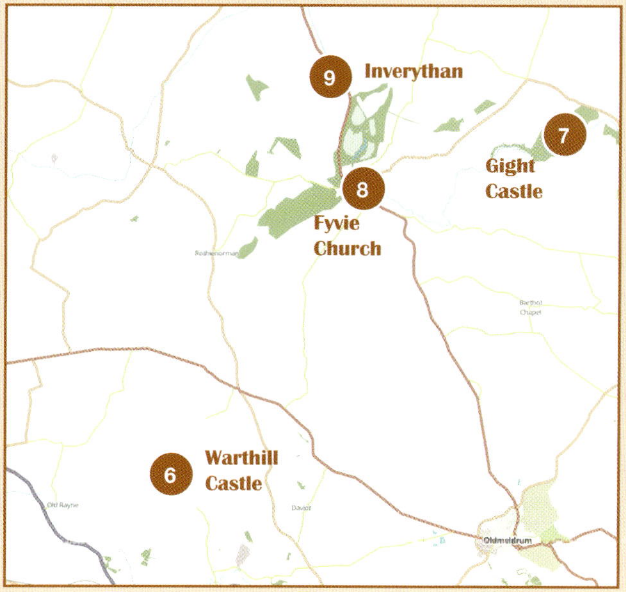
9 Inverythan
7
Gight Castle
8
Fyvie Church
6 Warthill Castle
Oldmeldrum

1. Taken by a Lion – Samuel Smart's Gravestone, Kintore Kirkyard, Kintore

As the snarling lion bore down on the exhausted trooper, did the thought of his wee Aberdeenshire village of Kintore run through the mind of Samuel Smart, destined to be a casualty of the Boer War? The faded gravestone of Archibald Smart and his family in Kintore Kirkyard mentions nothing of his grandson Samuel's dreadful fate, only that he was of Steinaecker's Horse and died at Komatipoort, South Africa, on 4 October 1900.

Major Von Steinaecker was a German soldier who had served as a lieutenant in the Prussian Army. After rapid promotion in the Colonial Scouts, which had been raised by the Natal government to deal with the threat from the Boers, Steinaecker formed his own elite group in March 1900, later known as 'Steinaecker's Horse'. They were a special operations team working for the Natal intelligence department. Thirty-four-year-old Samuel Smart was no fool, otherwise Steinaecker would not have recruited him.

The corps' first task was to blow up the bridge at Malelane in order to disrupt enemy communications. They would have to travel almost 400 miles from Eshowe, deep in Zulu territory, north to near Komatipoort, an area of swampland notorious for malaria. After a laborious two-month journey on which the men were sick and their horses died after contracting equine fever and being unable to eat, Steinaecker's men reached Nomahasha. They were given replacement horses and were guided by British settler, J. B. Holgate, who helped them avoid the heavily guarded bridge at Komatipoort and reaching Malelane by daylight. The bridge was successfully blown up and the team returned in triumph. From June until October, Steinaecker's Horse were based at Komatipoort, regularly fighting alongside the Zulus against the Boers. From 24 September, they pursued Boer rebel J.P. Coetzee's force of 300 men along the Selati railway. Holgate, now their chief scout, helped Steinaecker's Horse to locate their enemy at the Crocodile Bridge ranger post just beyond the Sabie River, a tributary of the Komati, where they engaged in a gun fight on 3 October. Five troopers were wounded.

Sabie River was in lion country. Perhaps the smell of blood had attracted a hungry female, perhaps Samuel Smart had disturbed a sleeping big cat, but the only information available comes from military researcher Bill Goldsworthy of Hamilton, New Zealand. The incident, which occurred on 4 October 1900, is recorded as follows: 'Trooper Smart taken that night by a lion.' He was mauled to death by the beast, while his fellow soldiers, eighty in number, went back down

the railway line. Smart's body was carried back the eight miles to Komatipoort. The news was eventually conveyed back to Kintore. His parents were dead and only his sister, Isabella Smart, was left. All she could do was record her brother's passing, knowing he could never return to Scotland. She died the following March, aged thirty-one.

2. Death in Thainstone Woods – Kintore Arms, Kintore

The Kintore Arms public house was the last place Mrs Anne Forbes visited before meeting her lover, George Stephen, a local woodcutter, for a tryst in the woods of the Thainstone estate near Inverurie in 1863. She was a frequent visitor to the Kintore Arms, a few miles from the wood, where she would buy a half-gill of whisky, drink one quarter before she met her paramour, and the other when she returned on her way home to her oblivious husband.

Anne and George were spotted by Mrs Duncan, a Kintore local, meeting outside the porter's lodge on the estate. Anne was laughing flirtatiously. Later in the day, George was observed walking from the woods carrying his axe, appearing completely at ease. A servant boy who worked for the estate came upon Anne lying in the undergrowth. She was in a state of undress, only her slip covering her body. Thinking her drunk, he approached tentatively, but as he came level with her, the boy saw her hair and face were drenched in blood, a horrible gaping wound in her head the cause. He screeched in terror and ran for his master. Soon the local constabulary and physician were on the scene. A contemporary report of the case noted: 'It was found she still breathed', an incredible situation considering her skull had been smashed open. The naïve Dr Aitken thought he could alleviate the pressure of the bone on her brain by removing the broken pieces. Anne's dying body was carried back to the porter's lodge; she never spoke another word.

The axe was found in George's kitchen, blood, hair and skin still clinging to the blade. He was arrested immediately and incarcerated in Aberdeen's East Prison. In April 1864, George pled guilty. His

defence immediately claimed that his client was in a state of insanity since the murder and could not coherently represent himself. The lawyer continued with an assassination of Mrs Forbes' character, reminding people of her drinking and her immoral behaviour. Incredibly, this defence was accepted. George would escape the rope. His response to his lawyer's masterful defence was less than grateful: 'Ah well, just a whiley langer to live.'

For six years he was a prisoner in the 'Asylum Ward' of Perth Prison, but in his sixty-seventh year, George Stephen died of 'epileptic insanity' a condition, which, according to the prison doctor, had been worse for the last month of his life. This begs the question, was it an epileptic fit that overtook George while he and Anne were cavorting in Thainstone woods? Whatever the case, the woods are now home to the grand Thainstone House Hotel and patrons are completely unaware of the brutal slaughter that took place within its grounds.

3. The Battle of Harlaw – Gilbert de Greenlaw's Grave Slab, Kinkell Chapel, Inverurie

A knight wears plate armour, chainmail and a helmet – the classic image we all associate with medieval warfare – yet this particular representation is featured on a grave slab in the ruins of Kinkell Church by the Ury's banks. This was Gilbert de Greenlaw as he was in life, riding into battle at Harlaw in 1411, never to return home alive. He was a cavalryman fighting for the Earl of Mar, the same Alexander Stewart who in the previous decade had seized his title by forced marriage to Countess Isabel Douglas. Mar was now a respected nobleman, keeping the peace in the Eastern Highlands, fighting in the king's name in Europe, lauded by chronicler Andrew Wyntoun as 'honest, able and elegant in person and behaviour'. Perhaps his new wife had calmed him down, or else he had now done all he needed to secure his position as a legitimate knight, despite his ignominious beginnings. Yet Mar went into battle against his cousin by marriage, Donald MacDonald, Lord of the Isles, over the Earldom of Ross. The latter was strategically important; it gave the Gaelic ruler a way into mainland Scotland, but equally gave the Lowland scoundrel control of the Highlands.

The whole situation turned on the crook-backed, thirteen-year-old Countess of Ross, Euphemia Leslie. Her late father's sister, Marion, was MacDonald's wife, but she was Mar's cousin through her mother, giving the two families a reason to fight. The Duke of Albany, Mar's uncle, had been trying to force the little girl to resign her title to his son, while she became a nun. Her disability meant she was not perceived as marriageable material.

By 1410, MacDonald gathered his fellow Gaels, a force numbering approximately 6,000, and descended on Dingwall and Inverness, leaving a trail of destruction in their wake. Word came to Mar that his Highland cousin intended to burn Aberdeen, thus at his Christmas dinner in Kildrummy, he gathered his most powerful friends, including Provost Robert Davidson of Aberdeen and Bishop Greenlaw, the uncle of Sir Gilbert. Mar promised he would defend the city from these Highland savages. Thus it was on 23 July 1411 that the Lowland army camped right below their enemies on farmland outside Inverurie between the farm touns of Harlaw and Balhalgardy, planning to attack MacDonald's men at dawn.

The dubby fields witnessed a slaughter like no other; many Lowland noblemen including Davidson and Greenlaw lost their lives for a conflict that ended with no obvious winner. Sir Gilbert had a coffin and a church burial, probably held by his sorrowing

kinsman, the bishop, yet most of the ordinary soldiers were simply buried on the battlefield. Centuries later, farmers would uncover mass graves indicating the level of casualties. Ultimately MacDonald's descendants would inherit Ross, making Harlaw the most dreadful waste of life over a family squabble.

4. The First Leslies of Inverurie – The Bass Motte, Inverurie Cemetery

Inverurie, a Celtic name meaning the confluence of the Ury, was reputed to originate from Nruri, the estate of local ninth-century chieftain, Grig, who occupied Dunnideer, the central fortress of the northern Picts. In AD 878, Grig defeated Aodh, son of Kenneth MacAlpin, King of Alba. Yet every generation brings more incomers; in Inverurie's case it was Bartolf, a highly intelligent and resourceful Hungarian aristocrat. The latter arrived in 1067 as follower of Margaret Aethling, whose brother Edgar was the last Saxon claimant to the English throne.

Malcolm Canmore, Margaret's new husband, rewarded Bartolf for his services with the lands of Lesselyn in the Garioch from which sprang their new family name of Leslie. Bartolf married Malcolm's sister, became constable of Edinburgh Castle and the queen's chamberlain. Bartolf's son, Malcolm Leslie, was made constable of Inverurie.

On the Bass, a fifty-foot high hillock consisting of glacial moraine, around AD 1070, Malcolm built the first wooden keep, the classic motte-and-bailey arrangement which the Normans had introduced to Britain after William the Conqueror's arrival in England. The Bass became the home of the Leslies and administrative centre for the Garioch. Victorian archaeologists discovered that the natural mound was scarped, i.e. cut away to create the motte, incorporate a wooden staircase and build a ditch around it for further defence. Finds such as worked flints and a stone adze suggested that the Bass had been occupied during both the Neolithic and Bronze Ages.

Norman and Malcolm, the sons of the first constable lived at the time of the Crusades. The younger son accompanied Malcolm Canmore's grandson, David, Earl of Huntington, to the Holy Land, never to return. Norman Leslie is recalled in the place name of Rothienorman, the prefix from the Gaelic word 'rath' meaning fort. The Leslies thus became one of the most powerful families in the district, building stone castles such as Leslie, Fetternear, Balquhain, Balgonie, Lickleyhead and Warthill.

By the fourteenth century, the Leslies were in great favour with the Bruces. Walter Leslie, son of Sir Alexander of Leslie Castle, was a crusader, and a soldier for the French, rewarded by Charles V with a pension for his pains. David II orchestrated the marriage of Walter and Euphemia, daughter of the last Celtic Earl of Ross, probably with a view to having his favourite gain the earldom. When her father died in 1372, Euphemia became Countess, and thus Walter the new earl 'jure uxoris' (Latin legal term, meaning 'by right of his wife'). Their son Alexander Leslie would inherit, going on to marry the Duke of Albany's daughter. Marion Leslie, Alexander's sister, meanwhile married Donald, Lord of the Isles, thus setting up the conflict which would lead to the Battle of Harlaw. The Bass was where the Earl of Mar is said to have marshalled his army before heading out to the battlefield.

5. Stone Sisters – Persephone and the Maiden Stone, Pitcaple

Hidden companion to the Maiden Stone, looking ancient, yet a flower-power dream of fairy-tale proportions, the statue of 'Persephone' stands in the grounds of a house near Pitcaple. Sculpted by Shaun Crampton in 1961, the statue is inspired by the nearby Pictish symbol stone, to which is attached the legend of the heiress of Balquhain, Mary Leslie, who lost a bet with the Devil and was turned to stone as she tried to escape. Persephone of course was the Greek beauty carried off by Pluto, King of the Underworld. She was allowed to return to earth for only half the year as she had eaten grape seeds while in Pluto's kingdom. Crampton's goddess carries a bunch of huge grapes in her right hand referencing that element of the tale, and a mirror in her left, echoing the mirror symbol on the Maiden Stone. Persephone's voluptuous figure is barely covered by the stone folds of her gown, perhaps dishevelled by her race back to the light and her mother Ceres, a corn goddess.

Scottish Travellers gave Persephone another identity, a Saracen maiden wronged by a Templar knight during the Crusades. Their story is an alternative reading of the ghostly legend set at Templars' Park, Maryculter. In the Travellers' interpretation, a Scots knight is wounded in battle and secretly cared for by the daughter of an Arab chief. Once the lusty knight is healed, he has a passionate affair with the girl and leaves her with child to the disgrace of her family. Back home in Aberdeenshire, the Templar is horrified when his Saracen lover turns up with her dead child in her arms. She has lost the baby in childbirth and comes to beg for his aid. In an act of desperate cowardice, the knight kills the maiden and buries her out near Bennachie, far from his Templar Chapel at Maryculter. During a church service, her ghost enters the sanctuary to accuse him of his wicked deeds, resulting in his immediate execution by the Master of the Temple.

The villain of this piece is quite unlike the brave and chivalrous Godfrey Wedderburn from the earlier tale, who although accused, never breaks his vow of chastity with the Saracen maiden. Local Traveller storyteller, the late Stanley Robertson saw Crampton's statue as the Saracen maiden's ghostly figure, coming to find her child's grave, represented by a sculpted urn which stands in the undergrowth directly opposite Persephone.

The towering statue was created from eight and a half tons of millstone grit, a form of coarse sandstone, whereas her companion, the Maiden Stone, was hewn of red granite. So they remain, calcified sisters united in their distress.

6. Gripping Fast on History – The Leslies of Warthill Castle, Whiteford, Pitcaple

Tabloid chatter and Aberdeenshire history do not often go together, but when Rose Leslie became famous for her role in the television series *Game of Thrones*, newspapers revelled in the fact that her parents lived in a medieval castle. Rose's father is Sebastian Leslie, 14th Laird of Warthill Castle, near Whiteford, Pitcaple. The family are descended from that same Hungarian nobleman who was brother-in-law to Malcolm III of Scotland.

The Leslies gained Warthill in 1518, through William Leslie of Wardes. His father, John, was the 2nd Baron of Wardes, whose family were a branch of the Leslies of Balquhain. William's second wife was Janet Cruickshank, the heiress of Warthill, whose grandfather Adam Cruickshank owned Little Warthill (sometime spelled 'Wartle') and 'two ploughgates of Harlaw' from 1482. William's first heir, John Leslie, had died at the Battle of Pinkie Cleugh in 1547, thus it was vital to have another son. Janet proved a very fertile mother, having twenty-one children, all marrying either their Leslie cousins, or into other important families such as Gordon, Lamb, Anderson and Lyall. The eldest, Adam Leslie was born in 1520.

The Leslies, like their neighbours the Gordons, were Catholic. They were 'out' for Bonnie Prince Charlie in the 1745 Jacobite Rebellion, but almost lost Warthill when a Hanoverian battalion was sent to raze it to the ground. The lady laird succeeded in bribing their captain to falsely report that he had burned the castle. The servants burned several large straw bales on the front lawn so it appeared to the soldiers' superiors, who observed the smoke from above the trees, that

Warthill was on fire and their orders had been carried out.

Warthill Castle itself has fourteenth-century origins, having been in the hands of the Balquhain Leslies since Robert the Bruce granted them 2,500 acres and the Hill of Foudland. 700 arable acres are still worked by a local tenant farmer. Sebastian explained that Warthill has technically never been sold since Bruce's grant, having been passed on by inheritance or marriage. The Warthill of the Balquhains would have consisted of one central square tower, which can be identified in the centre of the main entrance, surrounded by fairy-tale turrets from the Queen Anne period. The Victorian wing, dating from 1860, was demolished by Sebastian's father in 1968 as it was beyond repair by then. The initials of William Leslie, 9th Laird of Warthill, and Jane Anne Davidson, are engraved on central tower's roof pediments which feature a griffin, the family's heraldic device, and the Leslie motto, 'Grip Fast'. The latter originates from their Hungarian ancestor Bartolf, who, while fording a river on horseback with Queen Margaret, told her majesty to 'grip fast' on the reins for her own safety. The motto has proved apt to Warthill, which remains the Leslie family home to this day.

7. The Gordons of Gight – Gight Castle, Haddo Estate, Methlick

Gight, a name as curious and untameable as its inhabitants, translated as 'windy place' in Gaelic or 'chasm' in Norse, this was the home of the Formartine Gordons from 1479, when the estate was granted to the Earl of Huntly's third son. Thereafter, it seemed, ill luck beset the Gordons of Gight at every turn. The first laird was killed at the Battle of Flodden in 1513. His grandson, Alexander, was killed in a murderous duel with the Laird of Towie. The eighth laird fired upon his own house after a feud with his mother over his rights to Gight, and the last of the line, Catherine Gordon, lost her fortune to her drunken, profligate husband, Jack Byron. Many a gloomy prophecy was attached to the Gight family, and one said to have been fulfilled on the day of Catherine's marriage in 1785:

> When the Heron leaves the tree
> The Laird o' Gight shall landless be.

Catherine and Jack's son, George Gordon Byron, would of course go on to be one of Britain's foremost romantic poets, Lord Byron of Newstead Abbey. His father's family were equally wild. His great uncle, William Byron, from whom George inherited his title, was known as 'The Mad Lord Byron' because of his furious reaction to his son's marriage. Rather than let him inherit, William set about bankrupting the estate. The plan backfired when both son and grandson predeceased him, leaving another pile of debt for the already impoverished Gordon heir. Given his double dose of unhinged ancestry, it is perhaps not surprising that Lord Byron went to such excesses in his life

including having an affair with his half-sister Augusta, and embarking on his ill-fated foray into the Greek War of Independence.

Even before 'Mad Jack' charmed his way into Catherine's affections, Gight's fortunes were precarious. The story goes that just before the Covenanting army occupied the castle in 1644, the seventh laird, George Gordon, took his family's treasures and attached them to a great 'iron yett', presumably one of the gates from the castle, and had it sunk in a deep pool of the Ythan called the Hagberry Pot. Once the despised Presbyterian forces had finally gone, a servant dived into the river to retrieve the chest of booty. He surfaced empty-handed and declared that the treasure was safe, but in possession of 'the enemy of man'. His lordship sent the diver back to parley with the Devil for his goods, but after many agonising minutes, the drowned body surfaced, minus its head, the limbs floating independently of the torso.

The Earl of Aberdeen's son, Lord Haddo, occupied Gight after his father bought it to pay off some of his cousin Catherine's debts. But he too fell foul of Gight's curses, as he was killed in a riding accident in 1791. Gight was left to rot.

8. A Mother's Memorial – The Tiffany Window, Fyvie Kirk, Fyvie

A bereaved mother watches Irish glassmaker Frederick Wilson creating a heavenly vision of Archangel Michael at the factory of Louis Comfort Tiffany in New York. She weeps as it reminds her of her soldier son, Percy, who has died of typhoid fever during the Boer conflict in South Africa. She expresses the desire to have Wilson's finished product shipped back to Scotland and installed in the family church at Fyvie. Her friends know how much employment her husband has provided in America through his steelworks, now Illinois Steel Company, thus they buy her the glass out of appreciation.

Alexander Forbes-Leith, Percy's father, a former navy lieutenant, had acquired Fyvie in 1889 using his industrial fortune. Yet, as the grandson of Sandy Leith-Hay, one-time Lord of Leith Hall, Rhynie, Alexander was buying back a bit of local heritage. He and his American wife, Marie Louise January, had three children, yet only their son and elder daughter, Ethel-Louise survived. Percy was his mother's baby, the last of the three, born in 1881, thus it is no surprise that she was devastated when he succumbed to illness. Whether she drew comfort from the fact that as a 2nd Lieutenant in the 1st Royal Dragoons, nineteen-year-old Percy had not been killed as a result of enemy action, we cannot tell. What did give Mrs Forbes-Leith cause for concern was the realisation that Fyvie's Parish Church would have to be extended to cater for the beautiful new Tiffany window in Percy's memory. Money, however, was no object, thus in 1902 Alexander Forbes-Leith commissioned a brand new granite chancel and a family prayer loft for the kirk which itself was under a century old. The site itself, however, had been a place of worship dedicated to St. Peter since the late twelfth century.

Once finished, the fabulous window was finally revealed to the locals who could not fail to be impressed by the huge winged archangel in medieval armour, carrying a sword and a lance. Some might have wondered at the St. George's flag hanging behind Michael, yet as he was regarded as the patron of knights during the Middle Ages, it must be interpreted as the Crusaders' banner, not the English emblem. Michael stands atop the wheels of Time, representing the victory over Satan and the fallen angels before God created the world. The window is made of prism glass, allowing the colours to subtly change depending on the light behind them. Wilson remained in the US till his death, aiding Louis Tiffany in developing a foundation to support artistic talent,

leaving in 1923 to set up his own studio in Los Angeles. The only other Scottish church to have a Tiffany window is St. Cuthbert's, Edinburgh, which was installed in 1903, also to commemorate a Boer War soldier.

9. The Inverythan Bridge Disaster – Inverythan, Fyvie

'Telegraph to Aberdeen! The train is over the bridge at Inverythan!' gasped the breathless John Elder, under-gamekeeper at Hatton Castle, as he burst into the waiting room at Fyvie railway station on the evening of 27 November 1882. A whole year had passed without incident on the Great North of Scotland (GNSR) line, but that winter's night, the countryside heavy with snow, the Inverythan Bridge near Fyvie had collapsed, casting three freight wagons, the brake van and two passenger carriages off the rails and onto the roadway below, just clear of the river itself.

On returning to Inverythan, Elder and the other rescuers were met with total devastation. The engine and first class carriage were all that was left standing on the rails. The bridge was now a heap of rubble and mangled metal surmounted by the broken remains of carriages and wagons. Three and a quarter hours had elapsed since the accident and now at least the relief train could pull the engine back to Aberdeen, as well as transporting the bodies of the five who died. These terribly mutilated bodies had been extracted from the wreckage, covered and moved into neighbouring farmhouses or Fyvie Station to await transport. One of the dead was Free Kirk elder Gilbert Gilchrist, the highly esteemed forester of Cluny Castle, whom the *Aberdeen Weekly Journal* would later describe as 'a remarkable man for his intelligence and appreciation of letters', who left behind a wife and family.

Engine driver William Pratt gave the following evidence to the Board of Trade Enquiry: 'I have worked on this branch for about twenty-five years and I have never felt anything whatever wrong with this bridge.' He added that his engine and cars were in good order, having been checked on the morning of the disaster. After thorough examination, Pratt's words were found to be true; all the woodwork on the bridge was only eleven years old and in sturdy condition. The cause of the accident was the failure of a cast-iron girder on the east side of the bridge, which had snapped in half. Poor practice at the foundry meant the girder was not solid all the way through, reducing its tensile strength. The founders were cleared of blame as the fault would have been difficult to detect in a routine inspection. The Board of Trade recommended very strongly that in future the GNSR should use wrought-iron girders, which were more capable of bearing even the heaviest engines.

The Macduff/Banff branch line closed in 1966, rendering the Inverythan Bridge redundant. All that is left today are granite piers holding up the rusted remains of cast-iron panelling and girders. Yet there is nothing to show this was the place where five lives were lost on a winter's night in 1882 as result of shoddy workmanship.

KEMNAY TO CLASHINDARROCH

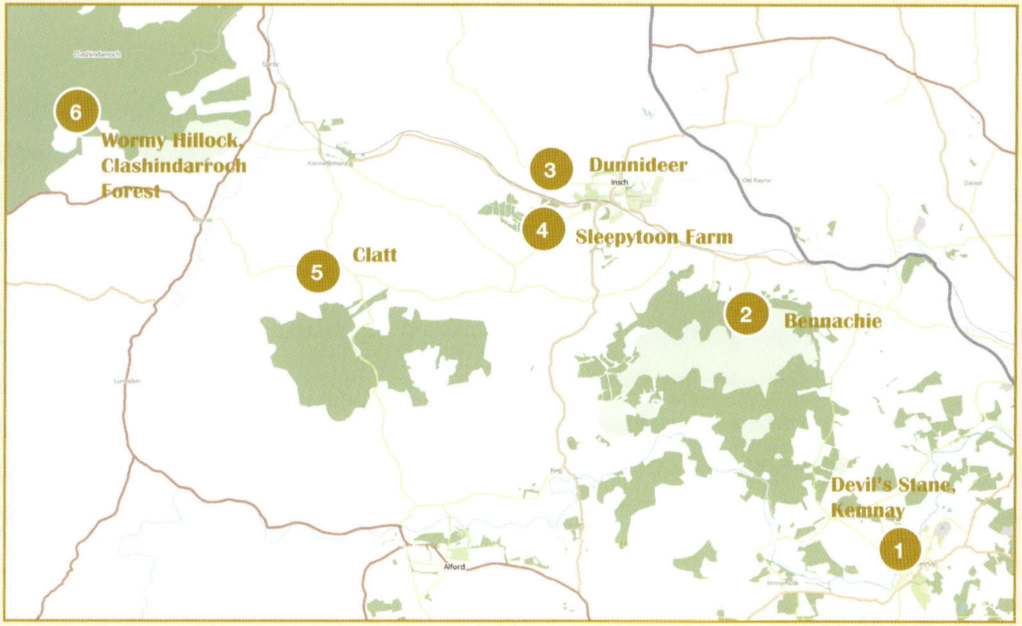

6
Wormy Hillock,
Clashindarroch
Forest
3
Dunnideer
Insch
4
Sleepytoon Farm
5
Clatt
2
Bennachie
Devil's Stane,
Kemnay
1
Alford

1. The Priest's Tale – The Devil's Stane, Greystones Road, Kemnay

The Devil seemed to have a particular dislike for the churchmen of the north east. Many are the tales of his attempts to frustrate their supplications against his evil ways, none more so than the priest of Kemnay. Greystones Road gives a little clue to the mysterious tale recorded in verse by Aberdeen poet William Cadenhead. In 1871, the Royal Society of Edinburgh, however, dismissed the story as a legend which attempted to explain how a 250-ton granite boulder could appear in a field seven miles from stones of the same type. No such granite was to be found in Kemnay, but the RSE members speculated that some 'natural agency', such as a glacier, could have brought the boulder to rest in the field near the old kirk.

Cadenhead sets the scene by describing the various 'spiritual champions' in the district, Culdee monks from Monymusk, Logie Durno and the bishop of Fetternear, but none compare with Kemnay's priest for 'lifting the downcast heart, for helping the lowly poor'. The poet continues by saying:

> On a' the bonnie banks o' Don
> There wasnae ane haly man
> Like him wha knelt in Kemnay kirk
> At the shrine o' our Ladie Anne

Saint Anne was the mother of the Virgin Mary; Kemnay's present Episcopal church is dedicated to her, yet it was the site of the present kirk where this devout priest was thought to have worshipped.

The Devil visits Bennachie – the latter described in terrible terms as 'ane o' the ports o' the byrnand pit', that is, a gateway to hell, which spewed fire at night – and is sent into a flaming rage by the Kemnay priest's good deeds. He curses the holy man and determines to kill him on the feast of St. Barnabas. The priest prays 'that Satan may forever be bound, to his dark and byrnand lair', perhaps aware of the spiritual warfare taking place around him. The kirk's organ plays out sacred praise, which reaches the Devil's ears on the mountain, driving him into further murderous paroxysms. He casts around for means to slay the troublesome priest, 'but nocht could he see save the bald grey rocks that glowered out through the heath'. Satan hoists one of the massive granite rocks in the air and throws it at the kirk roof. The rock is so big that its flight darkens the sky, causing the locals to flee in fear.

However, the priest's prayers and 'the power o' the sweet Sanct Anne' turn the rock aside in its path, causing it to land harmlessly in the field nearby. 'And there it sits in the kirklands yet, half-buried in the yird', writes Cadenhead, little guessing that the Devil's Stane would be surrounded by twenty-first-century housing many generations later.

2. The First Battle of Bennachie – Mons Graupius

‘We, the most distant dwellers on earth, the last of the free, have been shielded until today . . .’ roars Iron Age chieftain Calgacus to his assembled brethren as they are about to engage directly with the might of Rome on the slopes of Bennachie, the very border of their Highland territory. Stirred into a frenzy of bloodlust, the men begin to roar at their enemy, arrayed below in glistening bronze helmets and breastplates.

To the disciplined Roman soldiers, the sight of thousands of screaming Caledonians must have been at the very least a little unnerving. Yet our account of the battle of Mons Graupius is entirely from the victor’s perspective, penned by Roman poet Tacitus. It is he who gives Calgacus the rousing speech, invents the Caledonian leader’s name, which is Latin for ‘swordsman’, and probably vastly exaggerated the size of his army, all to praise his father-in-law, Gnaeus

Julius Agricola, Governor of Britain, who led the Roman force that day in AD 84.

Agricola’s aim was to smash the power of the Caledonian tribes of Highland Aberdeenshire and build a chain of defensive forts from Strathmore to the tip of the Grampians at Devana, i.e. Aberdeen. But the wily natives had continued to engage in guerrilla tactics, attacking the Romans in their marching camps overnight. They had raided the camp of the remote Ninth Legion, and would have slaughtered them all had Agricola's men not come to their rescue. The Roman general pushed on further into Caledonian territory, establishing temporary camps at Raedykes, Normandykes, Kintore and Durno, which drove the native leaders to call out all available warriors. Tacitus claims there were 30,000 Caledonians arranged along the slopes of Mons Graupius, the Mountain of Grampian, but battlefield historian Peter Marren suggests that even half this number would have been remarkable. The Romans numbered around 20,000, including infantry and cavalry from Rome, Europe and southern Britain.

The battle began as the Caledonians showered the Romans with stones and spears. Agricola sent forward his veteran forces, which hacked into the native line. Those Caledonians further up the hill charged down to encircle their enemy, but four cavalry forces met them, slicing them down with their short pointed swords. Mons Graupius descended into a rout and the Caledonians either fled or threw themselves upon their pursuers. By nightfall the Romans were mopping up, looting from the dead and killing any survivors. A few months later, before Agricola could consolidate his victory by entering Moray and Caithness, he was recalled to Rome and retired from active duty. Ancient warfare specialist Duncan B. Campbell speculated that Emperor Domitian felt that the Scottish invasion plan was an over-extension of troops in Britain and cost the Roman treasury far too much.

The Caledonians meanwhile breathed a sigh of relief as they were left alone, safe in the shadow of Bennachie, their Mons Graupius.

3. The Hill of Picts and Pagans – Dunnideer, Insch

Dunnideer was the seat of the Pictish chief, Grig, who defied the might of the new Irish/Gaelic dynasty in the form of Kenneth MacAlpin, by defeating and executing his son, Aodh, in AD 878. The conical hill commands an uninterrupted view of the surrounding countryside, including Bennachie, Hill of Christ's Kirk, Hill of Flinder and Tap o' Noth; there are a vast number of stone circles and some well-known Pictish symbol stones including the Picardy Stone which is directly north. Dunnideer's significance to pre-Christian religion is apparently such that it has been described as Scotland's Glastonbury Tor. Perhaps this accounts for a comment by fifteenth-century chronicler John Hardyng that King Arthur held circuit courts there.

The very name of Dunnideer could have supernatural origins. Nearby St. Drostan's Church in Insch suggests a linguistic link with Old Deer where the saint was reputed to have founded the church of Deer. The name meant 'Place of God'. The Gaelic word for a deity or god is 'Dia', thus the speakers of the Q-Celtic tongue could easily have named the site 'Dun-y-Dia', the Hill of God.

The site today has three walls of a thirteenth-century castle, including a full-height gable with a chancel window facing towards Tap o' Noth, the remains of a moss-covered vitrified fort which surrounds the castle and fragments of another outer wall, which would have created a triple system of defence for the occupants. Thus Grig's keep was quite rightly on a 'dun', but whether his god was of the old religion or the new, we cannot tell. Grig's treatment of Aodh MacKenneth suggests he was violently opposed to the faith of the Irish invaders.

David, Earl of Huntingdon and Garioch, as well as

friend of the Leslies of Balquhain, is believed to have built the first stone tower on Dunnideer in 1178. By the mid thirteenth century, Jocelyn de Balliol, born at Redcastle near Forfar, of an Anglo-Norman family, was laird of Dunnideer Castle. He is recorded in 1260 as granting to the Abbot of Lindores 'an annual sum and wayleave for a mill-lade from the Shevock Burn to the Mill of Insch', on condition that the abbot present Balliol and his heirs with a 'pair of white kid gloves every Whitsunday'. The close-packed style of the stonework in the remaining castle gable is very similar to that of Balliol's birthplace.

John Leslie, the sixteenth-century Abbot of Lindores before being made Bishop of Ross, describes Dunnideer as 'Dun o' d'or', 'Hill of Gold'. Certain spells cast at sunrise, could turn the hill to gold. Perhaps the bishop had seen the sun strike Dunnideer at dawn on a midsummer day, bathing it in golden rays of light and for a moment believed in magic. Dunnideer is definitely a treasure worth the visit.

4. Sleepytoon – The Farm of Christ's Kirk

'I agreed tae fee wi' him, an' thocht masel weel kent, until I got tae Sleepytoon, and there I did repent!' So run lines from Scots bothy ballad 'Sleepytoon', repopularised in the early 1990s by folk rock band Wolfstone. Bothy ballads were the farm workers' way of lauding good bosses, getting revenge on nasty ones or boasting of their often alcohol-fuelled adventures with female farm servants, or worse, the farmer's daughter! A bothy consisted of the living quarters for the male employees, usually at its most basic, with wooden box beds, straw-filled mattresses known locally as 'caff sakes', and a wood-fired stove for boiling water. A farmer who failed to provide decent lodgings for his staff or treated them with disdain was likely to find his reputation sealed by the balladeers whose songs would spread to the general populace at fairs and dances just as negative reviews of businesses are submitted to internet sites such as Trip Advisor in the present day.

This particular bothy ballad is associated with the eponymous farm at the foot of the Hill of Christ's Kirk between Kennethmont and Insch, beginning at the annual hiring fair. Sleepytoon's farmer Adam Mitchell promises light work, good food and decent pay, but the unlucky narrator soon discovers it is all a ploy to get cheap labour. The farm workers find themselves working long hours and being fined for leaving the farm, but they risk it to buy tobacco or 'court a lass'. The narrator admits that he was 'fined a croon for riding in the cairt' (in some versions, 'turnin' o'er the cairt'), but bears with Mitchell's poor treatment as he knows 'the term is nearly done, and soon we shall be free, and wi' that wary fairmer, I never mair will fee.'

Sleepytoon Farm was, previous to 1870, named

revels. Another ballad, 'Christ's Kirk on the Green', illustrates the wild goings-on at Sleepy Market: 'Was never in Scotland heard or seen, such dancing and deray . . . at Christ's Kirk on a day.' It was reputedly composed by King James V of Scots himself.

Adam Mitchell was the farmer from 1840 to 1858 while it was still named Christ's Kirk, after the hill on which the ancient Christ's Church of Rathmuriel had stood, dating from as early as the eleventh century. The annual Christ's Kirk fair was held on the church green until the late 1750s. It was nicknamed the Sleepy Market as it was held between dusk and dawn, usually ending in drunken Christ's Kirk Farm, thus the ballad owes its name more to the market than to the farm. The ballad's narrator ends by ridiculing Mitchell when they meet at a fair in Rhynie: 'I'll gie him a len' o' ma hankie, for tae dicht his snottery nose.' Sleepytown farm still exists today, but the bothies and fairs are a thing of the past.

5. Pagans and Popish Plots – Clatt Kirk, Clatt

Clatt's Celtic name means 'rocky outcrop'; locals used to pronounce it 'clate' indicating Gaelic would once have been their native tongue. The original site of Christian worship here was said to have been founded in AD 612, dedicated to Irish missionary, Saint Moluag. Associated with Lismore and Rosemarkie, this saint may have visited some time before his death in AD 592, and been able to converse with the locals, or perhaps they had visited one of his shrines and taken a liking to his particular brand of the new religion. He was no lowly monk, but an educated nobleman of Dalriada, the clan who settled in Argyllshire from the third century onwards, and his real name was Lughaidh, 'Moluagh' being a pet form of the name (Mo Luagh – my Luagh). Even more curious, his name is the same as Pagan god, Lugh the Long-Handed, reputedly the father of Ulster warrior, Cùchulainn and the leader of the Tuatha Dè Danann, one of the ancient tribes who occupied Ireland before the Gaels. A church dedicated to a saint with a Pagan name is odd enough, but one of Clatt's ministers had a controversial story of his own.

The lairds of Clatt were Gordons, based at Knockespock House, so it was no surprise that some of their ministers were of the same family. The Gordons of north-east Scotland, as we have seen in many of our stories, were staunch Catholics, and perhaps this explains the short-lived tenure of Rev. James Gordon (1583-93). His entry in the register of parish incumbents simply reads 'parson in 1583, proceeded against for treason in 1593.'

The record of court proceedings in Scotland for that year reveals that Rev. Gordon was summoned to answer charges of treason by James VI. He is cited along with some very weel-kent unrepentant Catholic noblemen including George Gordon, Earl of Huntly, Sir Patrick Gordon of Auchindoun, William Douglas, Earl of Angus and the infamous Francis Hay, Earl of Erroll. The latter had his castle at Slains blown up by the King for his involvement in the Spanish Blanks conspiracy. It would appear that James Gordon had become entangled with the plot, which involved a secret pact with Philip of Spain to restore Catholicism to Scotland.

Had he been mistaken for his namesake, a Jesuit priest and relative of Huntly's who was also involved? Clearly not, as he is described in the indictment as 'parson of Clatt'. Although Rev. Gordon and the others never appeared before the court, some were granted a royal pardon. But, nothing more is ever heard about James Gordon who would have had to flee Clatt, leaving his family and property behind. The pretty little kirk belies the drama that would have taken place when the royal messenger arrived with the summons in the spring of 1593.

6. Sleeping Dragon – Wormy Hillock Henge, Clashindarroch Forest

Legend has it that the prehistoric site Wormy Hillock is actually the buried corpse of a dragon who had molested the folk around Finglenny and was finally vanquished by some 'unknown St. George', according to local antiquarian James MacDonald in his 1891 book on the place names of Strathbogie. Standing on the hillock itself, which overlooks the curious earthen ring of dark heather and its central mound, it would be easy to imagine a curled up scaly body mouldering into the earth. Yet Wormy Hillock is no mythical 'worm' (the old word for a dragon), but a Stone Age henge monument, that is, a circular ceremonial site dating from the late Neolithic period.

The earliest settlers in Aberdeenshire were believed to have been at Balbride near Crathes, where excavations revealed the site of a large communal hall dating from 3800 BC. By the time Wormy Hillock henge was constructed, the beliefs and spiritual practices of the Neolithic people were changing. Communal burial cairns were giving way to cremation and burial of individuals within ditches and later stone circles. Henges were not so common here, thus Wormy Hillock could represent a particular sect with practices at variance with their neighbours. At only six metres across, our henge is very small in comparison with the huge Ring of Brodgar in Orkney, the Neolithic equivalent of a country chapel versus a metropolitan cathedral.

At Wormy Hillock and other similar sites, the outer ring contained a ditch which in turn enclosed an inner mound, which MacDonald speculated consisted of the earth excavated from the ditch. There is an 'entrance' from the lower ground on the riverbank which separated the henge from the ordinary land, emphasising its sacred status. Archaeologists designate Wormy Hillock one of the earlier or Class I henges due to this single entrance, as later sites had at least two, often aligned with winter and summer solstices. The siting of Wormy Hillock near Ealaiche Burn was also thought to be significant, as streams and rivers were sacred to these early people. There are also many ancient wells in this area, thus it is possible folk visited various sites for the worship of water spirits.

Henges and stone circles indicated new developments in both religious practices and design, as was evidenced by the highly-decorated 'Grooved Ware' pottery found at Balfarg Henge in Fife, dating from 3100 BC onwards. One of Balfarg's pots contained traces of the henbane plant, a relative of hemlock, which caused researchers to speculate as

to its use as a hallucinogen! Wormy Hillock's dragon legend might therefore have come from the fevered daydream of a prehistoric priest in a drug-induced trance. To later inhabitants the dragon story may have been simply a way of recognising it as a special site, the original reason having been lost by then.

KINGSWELLS TO CORGARFF

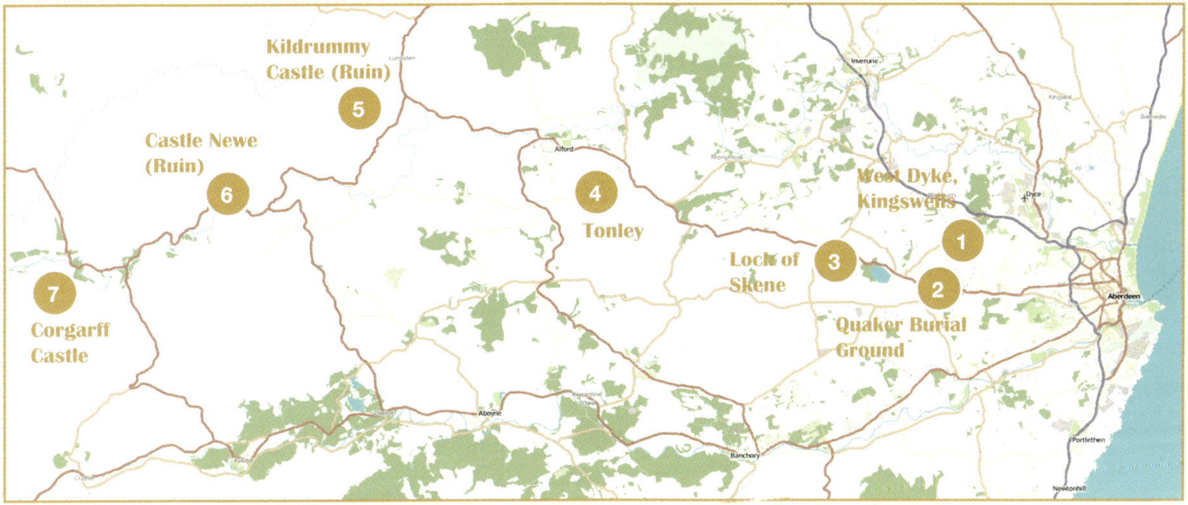
Kildrummy Castle (Ruin)
5
Castle Newe (Ruin)
6
4
Tonley
West Dyke, Kingswells
1
Loch of Skene
3
2
Quaker Burial Ground
7
Corgarff Castle
Inverurie
Alford
Monymusk
Dyce
Aberdeen
Aboyne
Banchory
Portlethen
Newtonhill

1. Raining Stones – The West or Broad Dyke of Kingswells

At the dawn of the Agricultural Revolution, the consumption dyke represented the most efficient use for excess stones by landowners who sought to enclose fields for crops. These stones were the remnants of the last Ice Age – great lumps of granite and sandstone, telling the story of our local geology. The West Dyke of Kingswells is one of the best remaining examples of a consumption dyke, credited to landlord Francis Edmonds from 1854. However, more recent research suggests the Edmonds merely added to the existing structure by creating a path atop it, wide enough to accommodate a horse carriage. In 1909, the minister of Newhills wrote to the *Aberdeen Journal*, praising Edmonds' work. The article described his 'laying a rough pavement of selected stones on the top, to have a dry elevated walk over that part of the property. This walk he continued eastward in a nicely shaped walk through a plantation to the limit of Kingswells Estate on the Goose Hill.'

Popular nineteenth-century author Catherine Sinclair wrote in 1840:

> You might fancy, in some parts of this county, that it rained stones instead of water! And towards the west, where rocks abound most, the superfluous stones are swallowed up in what is called an 'Aberdeenshire Dyke', built about six foot high and twenty or thirty feet broad, fit for a wagon to be driven on.

Although a children's writer, Catherine would have had an appreciation of land use through her father,

Sir John Sinclair, a keen exponent of the developments in agriculture with which he experimented on his Caithness estates. He was the man who, in 1791, invented the Statistical Account of Scotland – a forerunner of the British Census – which collated reports on all aspects of parish life from local churchmen, usually the most educated in their districts.

The whole concept of the consumption dyke was the easy disposal of these surplus rocks, rather than wasting time and money carting them away for sale. William Adam of Bucksburn, an advocate and landowner hit on an interesting variation. He constructed double walls at some distance apart and planted trees or hedges in the cavity between them. The trees would improve the drainage, drawing off water from the newly enclosed fields for their root systems. Long before actual pipes were used, this put the likes of Adam and Edmonds at the forefront of eighteenth-century land reclamation. As well as consumption dykes, the parish of Newhills used excess stones quarried from nearby fields to build the Church of Scotland which stands today.

The West or Broad Dyke represents a huge input of manual labour – it is 1,565 feet in length, thirty-three feet wide and six and a half feet in height. The dyke truly is an iconic feature of which the Kingswells folk can be justifiably proud.

2. In Silent Contemplation – Quaker Burial Ground, Kingswells/Westhill

Above a Kingswells farmhouse, surrounded by drystone walls is an anonymous little wild garden. The trees were planted by Francis Edmonds, the great agricultural improver of the nineteenth century, and golden daffodils waved peacefully the day I visited. But for a plaque on one of the trees, not a soul would know that this quiet plot was the Friends' Burying Ground. Better known as Quakers, the Religious Society of Friends, founded by George Fox during the English Civil War, sought to break away from the Established Churches of England and Scotland. The central tenet of their faith was the equality of all believers, which led them into great conflict with both religious and civil authorities.

Persecution was worst in Aberdeen – the local Quakers tried to bury their dead on land they had purchased in Gallowgate during the 1670s, but the council constantly disinterred the bodies and fined the families for 'improper burials'. Actions against Quakers had already begun in 1663 when the council banished George Keith, William Neper and William Stuart on pain of 'punishment in their bodies', Anyone found holding a Friends' meeting on their property would be fined 500 Scots merks. It was believed that by 1670, at some point or other, almost every local adult male member of the Friends had been imprisoned in the Aberdeen Tolbooth. They tried to preach from the windows, which were blocked up to prevent their message of non-conformism reaching the public. Quakers were banned from becoming burgesses, meaning they could not own land in Aberdeen nor lawfully enter trade.

Lilias Skene, who is commemorated by a plaque on the wall of Aberdeen's Crown Street Friends' Meeting House, was also buried there alongside her husband, Alexander Skene, Baillie of Aberdeen. She wrote in defence of her faith, the following words making clear the Quaker love of equality:

Many of the city's prominent men became Quakers, including Alexander Jaffray, landlord of Kingswells from 1610. He was able to create a safe burial site for his family and fellow adherents. Rejecting traditional gravestones, the Friends preferred to have no marker for the dead, believing that they would be reunited in Heaven, and thus should only be remembered in prayer. The Friends' Burying Ground at Kingswells contains Jaffray himself, who died in 1673, his daughter, Lilias, and his wife, Sarah Cant, the sister of staunch Presbyterian preacher, Andrew Cant. Quaker poet

One life, one love, one peace, one joy, one way,
One in our principles, our strength our stay.
One mark, one prize, one hope, one expectation,
One crown of glory, one complete consolation.
In life, in death, in bonds, at liberty
In Christ we're one, O glorious mystery.

The last Quaker to be interred in Jaffray's burial ground was Robert Melvin, a weaver, who died in 1808.

3. The Wizard Laird's Date with the Devil – Loch of Skene

The shimmery waters on Loch of Skene hide a dark secret – the fate of the erstwhile laird, Alexander Skene. Skene, sixteenth of that ilk, lived around 1680 to 1724, a time when superstition was still rife all over Europe, despite the supposed enlightenment of the Reformation. The laird was believed to have attended the University of Padua in Northern Italy, reputed to offer such arcane subjects as necromancy and astronomy. When Skene returned, the word was he had become a student of the Devil himself.

Skene was reputed to possess the power to 'reest' anyone who annoyed him – in other words, he could either force them to remain rooted to the spot, or bend their will to his own. A local ceilidh got on Skene's nerves so much he cast a spell on the dancers so they kept going until their feet bled and they cried in agony.

The 'Wizard Laird' as he was known, was always accompanied by crows and ravens, the birds of ill omen. One night, he instructed his coachman, Kilgour, to ride the coach and horses across the Loch of Skene, but not to look around at the laird's passenger. That night was All Hallow's Eve, when the spirits of the dead are free to wander and witches dance in praise of their dark master.

The loch was frozen, so Kilgour fancied his chances. He waited at the water's edge as his master and the unknown passenger climbed into the black coach behind him. He cracked the whip and the two horses trotted onto the sheet ice.

Hearing the low whispers, Kilgour couldn't contain his curiosity, and turned to see Alexander and 'Auld Cloven Hoddie', the Earl of Hell himself, deep in conversation! The Devil had come to visit his new recruit, and Kilgour suddenly realised he was riding the heavy coach into the middle of the frozen loch. The Evil One turned his gaze on the poor coachman, who froze in terror, dropping the reins – horses, coach, and all sunk to the bottom of the loch and neither Kilgour, nor the Wizard Laird were seen again.

However, Alexander Skene is afforded a grand tomb in the grounds of his house. His former tenants feared him as much dead as they did when he was alive. Every Halloween from then on, the people built bonfires and prayed that the purifying fire would protect them from the wizard's ghost.

The loch of Skene still exists today on the road to Banchory, and the gatehouses of the Skene estate are in a prominent position by the water's edge as they were in Alexander's day. His line died out with the twentieth laird in the 1800s, but local folk are still wary of the Wizard Laird's return should the loch waters ever freeze solid!

4. Growing Old Disgracefully – Patrick Byres of Tonley House, Kirkton of Tough

'My father what? Had a duel? He's in his seventies! Silly man!' So might James Byres of Tonley have exclaimed when he was brought word about the unseemly quarrel occasioned by Byres Senior. Patrick Byres was an Irish Jacobite, born in Dublin in 1713. In 1741 he married Janet Moir of Stoneywood and became a Burgess of Guild in Aberdeen, yet his political leanings and hot Celtic temper seem to have constantly landed Patrick in trouble.

His first problem was his involvement in the 1745 Rebellion, fighting on Bonnie Prince Charlie's side as Major Byres in Stoneywood's regiment. Escaping Culloden, Patrick's ally, Gordon of Cluny, hid him in his castle until he and his family escaped to France. He managed to hang on to Tonley by the clever suggestion that his English name was Peter, thus he was not Patrick Byres the rebel. While his youngest sons, William and John, developed military careers in the navy and Royal Engineers respectively and his second son, Robert, took up merchant interests in Prussia, the eldest, James, became something of a tour guide. He embraced antiquarian studies in Rome and became the go-to ex-pat for visiting Scots gentlefolk on their 'grand tours' of Europe. Meanwhile, his father returned to Tonley, Mrs Byres hoping her husband's adventures were over. But, thanks to Janet's nephew, James Abernethy of Mayen, Patrick was to become the centre of unwanted attention once more in 1763. A traditional ballad is dedicated to the incident in which John Leith of Leith Hall, Rhynie, was murdered by Abernethy after an argument in the New Inn, Aberdeen.

It was the Martinmas or winter term when debts were settled. According to the ballad, 'four and twenty gentlemen sat birling at the wine'. As is often the case 'fan drink's in, wit's oot', and the Laird of Mayen cast up an old grudge to John Leith. The latter gave him as good as he got, whereupon Abernethy left. Patrick Byres would later reveal that his nephew had gone to fetch pistols in order to settle the matter with a duel to which Leith had agreed. A few of them had talked long into the night without the weapons leaving the table, yet soon after, shots shattered the early morning peace of the Castlegate and Leith's servant found him bleeding to death in the street. James Abernethy had fled on a horse provided by his uncle, never to return. Many believed Patrick had egged James on, providing both weapon and escape route, but he denied it. The Leiths never forgot.

The spat at Bridge of Alford decades later was with Alexander Leith of Glenkindie, over the siting of a new road. Patrick's friends calmed the pensioner down and sent him home to Tonley and likely to a reprimand from his son James.

5. Blood Wedding – Isabel of Mar and Kildrummy Castle

In 1404, there was no woman as isolated as Isabel Douglas. Her brother, eminent knight, James, Earl of Douglas and Mar had been killed at the battle of Otterburn in 1388. The Scots king, Robert III was too old and sickly to be of any support to her, and his brother, Robert, Duke of Albany was now absolute ruler of the country. To crown her sorrows, Isabel's husband, Malcolm, was dead, reputedly murdered by Alexander Stewart, son of the infamous 'Wolf of Badenoch'. Isabel and her castle at Kildrummy were apparently next on his list to conquer.

The only real power a medieval noblewoman could wield was through her possessions. On the death of her brother, in the absence of any legitimate male heirs, Isabel was made Countess of Mar and thus Châtelaine of Kildrummy Castle. She was the most eligible lady in the kingdom and by 1384, she was married to Malcolm Drummond, the equally powerful Earl of Lennox's son, brother-in-law to Robert III, and nephew of Margaret Drummond, David II's queen. Yet in their relatively peaceful eighteen-year marriage, Isabel never had a child, possibly because her husband spent so much time away on court business. This was when Alexander Stewart took advantage – it is believed he was the originator of an attack by the Stewarts of Appin on Stobhall Castle, Drummond's clan seat, which ended in Malcolm's death in his own dungeon in 1402. Alexander's attack on Kildrummy came quickly after. Despite Isabel's knights fighting hard to protect her and her castle, it fell to the rapacious Stewart nobleman and his gang of thugs.

Neither King Robert nor his brother, Albany, made

any attempt to punish their nephew for his deeds, when ordinarily such behaviour would have seen Alexander's head on the execution block. The king was sick and no longer able to cope with his duties; his brother was a firm ally of Alexander and happy to collude in his power-grabbing scheme.

Then Alexander carried out a spectacularly astute but cruel gesture; having left Kildrummy, he returned with the Bishop of Ross and most of Isabel's tenants to the barbican of the castle. Isabel came to the gate and Alexander replaced the keys of the castle, which he had stolen, into her hands, saying he did so freely with a good heart, for her to dispose of them as she saw fit. Looking down on the kneeling figure, Isabel saw only her husband's killer, but in fear of her life she stated publicly that she willingly would take Alexander as her husband and give to him as her dowry her earldom and lands. She then signed away her rights and lived the last four years of her life a prisoner. Alexander

promptly remarried a Belgian heiress. Isabel's revenge came from beyond the grave when Alexander's line died with him and James I claimed the earldom and Kildrummy for the crown in 1435.

6. Bombay Jock's Legacy – Castle Newe, Strathdon

'For sale – 200 splendid doors of all sizes, 120 windows, wood and marble mantelpieces, etc': this advertisement appeared in the *Press and Journal* on 27 March 1927. It referred to the demolition of Castle Newe, once the seat of Baronet Forbes, built in 1831 by Aberdeen's foremost architect, Archibald Simpson. The Provost of Banchory was the seller, having bought the property from Charles Stewart Forbes, 5th Baronet, who reluctantly had to divide up his ancestor Charles Forbes' estate.

Castle Newe would never have existed without the success of Sir John Forbes of Newe, also known as 'Bombay Jock', Charles' paternal uncle and benefactor. Born in 1743, having seen his homeland devastated in the aftermath of Culloden, John went to work for the East India Company in 1764. By 1767, he was authorised by his employers as a 'free merchant'

of India and allowed to build up his own business. Such was Jock's success that Forbes Gokak Ltd. is today the oldest Scottish-Asian company in the world. As well as using his fortune to beautify his adopted home in Mumbai, including building the Town Hall and Royal Asiatic Society Library, Jock's mission was to revitalise his native county of Strathdon, thus endearing himself forever to his fellow countrymen. He was praised by the local minister for the 'vast improvement of the country', funding the drainage and enclosing of fields, erection of bridges and turnpike roads, and comfortable houses for his tenants, in a similar fashion to William Cunliffe Brooks of Glen Tanar. But more importantly, Bombay Jock's fortune had allowed him to regain his ancestor Lord Alexander Forbes of Pitsligo's lands which had been attainted after Culloden. It paved the way for his nephew Charles to receive a baronetcy in 1823.

Charles had worked for his uncle, but returned to Britain to enter politics in 1811. On receiving his honour, he in turn created the Lonach Highlanders and the famous Lonach Gathering. The intention was 'to preserve the Highland dress . . . the Celtic tongue and support loyal, peaceable and manly conduct, and to promote social and benevolent feelings amongst the inhabitants of the district'. The Lonach Society built the Baronet's Cairn on Lonach Hill in thanks to Sir Charles. Next on Charles' agenda was to further commemorate Bombay Jock by employing Archibald Simpson to create a castle fit for the descendants of Lord Pitsligo. It was to be the 'palace of the peak', standing 898 feet above sea level on a verdant lawn sloping down to the Don, surrounded by ancient trees.

Sadly, despite the Forbes's great efforts, all that remains of Castle Newe is a tiny fragment on the road to the present House of Newe. However, another architect would salvage the freestone blocks and use them in the medieval pastiche that is Elphinstone Hall, built by Alexander Marshall Mackenzie in 1927.

7. Edom o' Gordon and the Massacre of Corgarff – Corgarff Castle, Strathdon

Corgarff Castle stands white and sentinel-like above the Don, a symbol of the area's warlike past. Its star-shaped curtain wall was added in 1746 when it was occupied by English troops, remaining in their possession until 1831. Originally the Earl of Mar's hunting lodge, Corgarff was Forbes of Towie's family seat during the reign of Mary, Queen of Scots. 1571 was the year Margaret Campbell, wife of John Forbes, defended Corgarff with her life. The ballad 'Edom o' Gordon' records her vow to her terrified children:

> I winna gie up my house, my dear
> To nae sic traitor as he
> Come weel, come wae, my jewels fair
> Ye maun tak your share wi me.

Forbes was absent from home when Adam Gordon, the fourth son of the Earl of Huntly came with murder in mind. Some historical accounts suggest it was Gordon's deputy, a Captain Kerr who set fire to the castle with the express purpose of killing the family.

The Protestant Forbes and Catholic Gordons had hated each other for years. The Forbes clan had just defeated the Gordons in two earlier battles at Tillyangus and Craibstone, thus retaliation was inevitable. Adam Gordon, who had witnessed the execution of his brother John in Aberdeen for his part in the Battle of Corrichie, was to be the author of that vengeance. Whether Adam himself or Kerr ordered the burning of Corgarff, we cannot be sure, but the ballad sets Gordon up as the villain. According to 'Edom o' Gordon', Margaret sees soldiers riding towards the lonely Donside fortress on a dark winter night and mistakes them for her husband's men. When she puts on a good frock and has the table set, she is horrified to discover her mistake. Margaret tries to reason sweetly with Adam Gordon, who wickedly suggests she should come down and be his bedfellow for the night. In her rage at this insult, she fires a pistol at his heart, but sadly misses, igniting Adam's rage against her and prompting him to order the castle to be burnt. Too late, John Forbes returns to the blackened mass of bodies, but, according to the ballad, succeeds in attacking the vanguard of Gordons and killing a few for good measure.

According to sixteenth-century Scots court records, Forbes entered two complaints against Gordon in 1573 and 1578, both referring to the Corgarff massacre, saying that his house, wife and bairns 'were all utterly wrackit and brunt'. Years later, the Crown and Parliament finally forced the warring families to make peace. Corgarff was rebuilt, but would be razed again by the Jacobites to prevent it being occupied by Government troops and then seized from John Erskine, Earl of Mar, in 1715 before returning to the Forbes family. Now a museum, the castle guards only fields of sheep, where once the vengeful Gordons gathered.

HILL OF FARE TO CORSE

Macbeth's
Cairn, Perkhill
3
Auld Craobhie,
Lumphanan
Drove Road
2
Corrichie
Memorial
1
Beltie Road

1. Remember the Day of Corrichie – Hill of Fare, B977 Garlogie to Raemoir

The Earl of Huntly, elderly George Gordon, sat atop his horse just outside Garlogie at dawn on 28 October 1562, ready to do battle with his enemy, James Stewart, half-brother of Mary, Queen of Scots. Stewart had recently been designated Earl of Moray and Mar by the Queen, much to the annoyance of Huntly, who regarded these regions as his. But the final straw for the old man was the outlawing of his third son, Sir John Gordon, who had already been imprisoned for attempted murder, now a fugitive under his father's protection.

Huntly had been confident of support from his traditional allies, boasting he could gather a force of 20,000, but the men behind him numbered little more than 500. Stewart's superior army attacked at first light, chasing the Gordons all the way to Meikle Tap, and down in the boggy hollow of Corrichie, which translates from Gaelic as 'heathery howe' where they were quickly routed. Huntly, realising his cause was lost, apparently surrendered his sword to Andrew Redpath, Queen Mary's bodyguard. Huntly then fell from his saddle, and according to English Ambassador Thomas Randolph, who would later report the events to Elizabeth I, Huntly 'bristit and swelt, so that he spak not ane word'. Historians speculate that the old earl either died of a stroke or heart failure.

It was John Gordon who was left to bear the full force of the Queen's ire against this once powerful Catholic family. He would confess proudly of his plan to kill the new Earl of Moray and marry Mary, establishing a new Catholic dynasty. John's ill-advised rebellion would end in his bloody beheading in Castlegate below the window of Earl Marischal Keith's house where Mary and her half-brother were staying. The inept executioner apparently had to hack at John's neck with an axe three times before parting the head from his shoulders, flooding the cobbled street with blood in the process. Thus with the Battle of Corrichie died the hopes of a Catholic restoration. This suited Mary, determining to endear herself to the English Protestants in hopes that they might accept her as a successor to her cousin Elizabeth, still the 'Virgin Queen'. Four years later, the Gordons would be back in favour and Mary would be married to her Catholic cousin, Henry Stewart, the ill-fated Lord Darnley. James Stewart would no longer have control over his half-sister's actions.

A lonely granite obelisk erected by the Deeside Field Club in 1951 on the B977 Garlogie to Raemoir road is all that remains today to mark the site of the battle. Inscribed on the side facing the road are the Gaelic words 'Cuimhnichibh La Coire Fhraochidh' ('Remember the Day of Corrichie'), and on the rear is a bronze plaque describing the battle. Blink and you might miss it!

2. Tales of the Travelling Folk – Auld Craobhie and the Old Road of Lumphanan

Auld Craobhie is a 200-year-old oak tree loved by Stanley Robertson, master storyteller and singer of the Scottish Travelling community. Stanley's cultural education took place 'on the Auld Road', an old drove track above Lumphanan, which Travellers journeyed upon every summer to hawk home-made metal goods, meet with their kin and tell stories.

To Stanley, Craobhie was the Tree of Life. His mother often told him 'this wis the best tree in aa the wid' and that if he lived a good life, he would 'grow up fine and strang like this tree'. The Robertsons and Stewarts, cousins all, would camp near Auld Craobhie's boughs. The tree and the road itself were imbued with supernatural qualities not least because of their proximity to Macbeth's Cairn. Many were the stories that young Stanley heard and would later preserve in his book of Traveller tales, *Exodus to Alford.*

The road began just past the old Parish Church of Lumphanan, the kirkyard gate being somewhere that Stanley and other Traveller children would fearfully avoid. They knew the tale of Rob Haa, the tinsmith who entered the kirkyard at night only to be possessed by the spirit of an evil laird, intent on vengeance. A Traveller woman of the MacPhee clan found herself attacked by a horrible skeletal phantom clad in a black cloak, whom she met on the Auld Road. When her husband, Willie, a bare-knuckle fighter investigated, he was beaten so severely by the same entity, he was hospitalised.

Auld Craobhie himself had his own tale concerning the treasure hidden beneath his roots. In one of the many 'Jack' stories, the eponymous hero is a poor shepherd with a widowed mother. His master is 'hunger's grandfaither', i.e. extremely parsimonious. Both Jack and the laird discover that a special event will occur on Midsummer's Eve – Auld Craobhie, king of the oaks, will rise up and dance with his attendant trees by the river, leaving their 'birthspots' open. These were all filled with the jewels and wealth of the earth. The promise of riches sends both Jack and the laird to investigate, the latter threatening Jack's life if he dares go near Craobhie's deep well of booty. But the wise shepherd takes only enough to pull his mother and himself out of poverty, and is able to escape the birthspot of a smaller tree by the help of the laird's servant girl and a ladder knitted from scrap wool by his mother. The greedy laird ignores their pleas to help him, as he continues to fill his pockets with gems. Auld Craobhie returns to his birthspot, crushing the laird to death.

Auld Craobhie stands today, his boughs reaching out in friendship to all who will greet him, guarding the Auld Road and its hidden tales of wonder and horror.

3. The Real Macbeth – Macbeth's Cairn, Perkhill, Lumphanan

The king's terrified servants wrap his decapitated body in their cloaks and carry it up the hill to a sacred site above Lumphanan. They hastily bury Macbeth, intending to return after nightfall to transport the royal corpse to its final resting place on the holy island of Iona.

In 1057 the real Macbeth was killed because he stood in the way of Malcolm Canmore, son of the previous king, Duncan, claiming the throne of Alba. Duncan was hardly the meek, elderly king of the play, but rather a vicious bully who killed off his royal competition – Macbeth's father and his cousin. Macbeth, however, according to Irish/Gaelic sources, was 'fair, yellow-haired and tall', and secure enough in his seventeen-year reign to make a pilgrimage to Rome in 1050, where he 'scattered money like seed to the poor'. Far from being a usurper, Macbeth and his wife, Gruoch, were descendants of the previous kings of Alba, Malcolm II and Kenneth III.

The 'Scottish Play' with which we are all familiar, is in fact a total reversal of the truth, written to please James VI who had recently become James I of a new United Kingdom. Shakespeare appealed to James' obsession with witchcraft and the supernatural, weaving a romantic origin for the Stuarts in Banquo whom the witches prophesy, 'Thou wilt get kings, though thou be none.' The play proved one of the most popular of Shakespeare's 'histories' despite it being mostly pro-Stuart fiction. So why did the Bard get it so wrong? His main historical source, Raphael Holinshed, was relying on misleading accounts of Macbeth written over centuries as Celtic Alba evolved into Anglo-Norman

Scotland. The real tragedy is that these accounts were written by Scottish chroniclers from a time when the Stuart dynasty was in the ascendancy.

Three centuries after Macbeth's reign, John of Fordun's *Scotichronicon* describes Duncan's death in battle as murder and invents the character of Macduff as a former friend of Macbeth. Andrew of Wyntoun, writing forty years later, weaves a vile fairy tale, introducing the witches, Macduff's charm as 'the knight who was never born' and describes Macbeth as a 'son of the Devil'. Hector Boece, Principal of King's College, Aberdeen, writing in the 1500s, further adds the characters of Banquo and Lady Macbeth and states that Macbeth kills Macduff's family. Thus the lie was complete!

Macbeth's reign ended in a bloody skirmish outside Lumphanan, when Malcolm slew him in hand-to-hand combat and cut off his head as a trophy. The queen placed her son, Lulach on the throne, only for him also to be murdered by Malcolm Canmore, who finally secured the kingdom in 1058. The cairn that served as Macbeth's temporary tomb was excavated in 1855 and is likely to have been a prehistoric cist burial. No bones remain today.

4. Johnny Milne of Tillyskukie: Aberdeen's Last Hangman – Tillyskukie Farm, Corse

Within sight of Corse Castle, the seat of the Forbes family, stands the farm of Tillyskukie. Apart from its odd name, meaning 'clumsy hillock', it is weel kent for its association with Aberdeen's last hangman, Johnny Milne. He was an itinerant farm labourer who was caught stealing valuable beehives from the Corse estate. Johnny landed in Aberdeen's Tolbooth, where he faced seven years' transportation for larceny. However, Johnny found a way to save his skin by offering to take on the job of civic executioner which had been vacant for a year since the death of the previous incumbent, Jock McDonald. His offer was readily accepted by the grateful magistrates. Johnny's wife, the formidable Christian Milne née Waters, would have been delighted about her husband's new civic appointment, especially as it came with a wage, a free house, certain free perks from the market, as well as grazing for their pony. Mrs Milne apparently ruled the roost at home, thus being made public 'Hangie' was a huge ego-boost for this craven little man who appears in an 1806 painting of the Castlegate wearing a blue jacket and a red tam o' shanter bonnet. But Johnny reckoned without the power of the mob, when his first execution in 1810 almost became his last!

Andrew Hosack was sentenced to hang for theft, but the assembled crowd believed the rumour that he was actually guilty of the brutal murder of a crofter and his daughter near Keith in 1797. Murderers' bodies were handed over to the anatomy surgeons in Marischal College for dissection as part of their sentence; thieves were only hanged then given a pauper's burial. The roar went up as Hosack throttled

at the end of the rope on the gallows facing down Marischal Street: 'Send Hosack tae the surgeons!' Johnny cut down the corpse once Hosack's legs had finally stopped kicking, but every cart in the city had been hidden to prevent him transporting the rough wooden coffin to the Broadhill for burial, such was the public's desire to see the apparent murderer properly punished. After entreating his fellow citizens to show some respect, Johnny continued to be shouted down, whereupon he resigned, much to the chagrin of the magistrates. Johnny was eventually persuaded to repent of his hasty decision, most likely by his angry wife, but Hosack's corpse ended up at Marischal after all, being stolen from its shallow grave. Johnny's career as hangman continued without major incident until his death in 1831. Two years later, the city abolished the office of hangman, leaving Christian Milne and her daughter homeless. At least Johnny had provided a decent living for them for two decades, making a better hangman than a labourer or thief, with which his former employers at Tillyskukie might have readily agreed.

ROTHIEMAY TO DRUMDELGIE

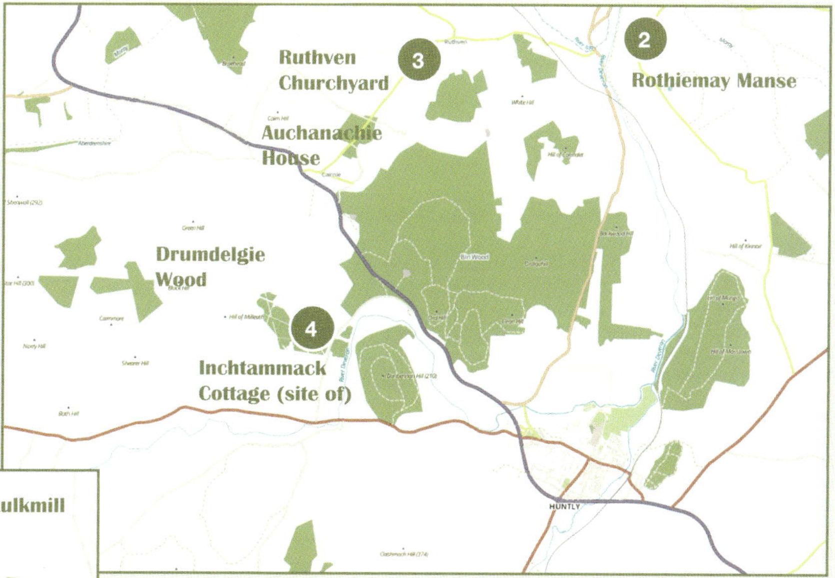

Ruthven Churchyard
3
2
Rothiemay Manse
Auchanachie House
Drumdelgie Wood
4
Inchtammack Cottage (site of)
HUNTLY

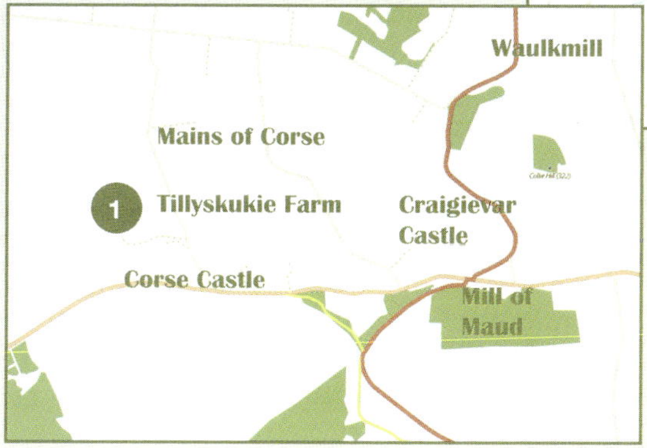

Waulkmill
Mains of Corse
1
Tillyskukie Farm
Craigievar Castle
Corse Castle
Mill of Maud

1. Parson Gordon: Map Maker and Minister – Rothiemay Manse

'A silver cup, a silk hat and ane silk gown for his bed-fellow' was the reward given to Parson James Gordon of Rothiemay and his first wife Margaret for drawing up what is now Aberdeen's earliest known illustrated map in 1661. James inherited his skill in geographical surveying from his father, Robert Gordon of Straloch, famed cartographer, musician, mathematician and antiquarian. In fact, the Church of Scotland seemed to be fairly supportive of James' extra-curricular activities – he was released from ministerial duties in 1642 to complete a new map of Fife. Because the Kirk had already agreed to the petition of Privy Councillor, Sir John Scot, to carry out surveys of all their parishes, it made sense to employ such a skilful man as James Gordon.

The 1661 Aberdeen survey demonstrates the parson's skill as an artist, as he adds clear representations of King's College in its original form and a 'prospect of New Aberdeen' in which the spires of St Nicholas Kirk, the Tolbooth and the windmill of Gallowgate are instantly recognisable. James had previously drawn up an Edinburgh map, being paid 500 Scots merks and becoming a burgess of the city for his pains. However, the parson was furious with the engraver, De Witt, for falsifying the scale of the city sketches, believing that the latter had done it 'to make [the maps] sell dearer'. Following Edinburgh, Parson Gordon continued with his Fifeshire survey.

James Gordon, born in 1617 at Pitlurg, the fifth of eleven boys, was appointed minister to Rothiemay Parish in 1641. He was not always so popular with his ecclesiastical employers due to his views on the National Covenant. The previous incumbent, Rev. Alexander Innes, had been dismissed and transferred to another parish for refusing to sign, but James admitted in his own diaries that he 'ran the hazard oftener than once of being turned out of that place', as he preferred the Episcopal form of church governance to the new Presbyterian one which, in this period, was being forced hard upon the populace. James found himself censured several times for his unwillingness to 'exercise discipline' against those who were more overt in their anti-Presbyterian attitudes. It is unsurprising that the parson was of a more conservative persuasion, having been brought up in a Jacobite household on close terms with the Catholic Gordons of Huntly. James penned his own account of the times, *Memoirs of Scots Affairs 1620-51*, published in 1661.

With six children, his sons all from his second marriage, James would have had a pleasant life at Rothiemay Manse, working alternately on his maps and sermons. Sadly, James' father Robert never saw the masterful survey of Aberdeen, dying two months before publication. Yet James' third son, Ludovick Gordon, would succeed him as minister of Rothiemay in 1680.

2. Ruthven's Bloody Past – Auchanachie House and Ruthven Kirkyard

Thomas Gordon of Ruthven, better known as 'Tam o' Riven', made a fearsome sight arrayed in armour and saddled on his grey charger. His cause was the disputed ownership of Balloch Hill, which stood at the boundary between his lands and the Barony of Grange, which belonged to the Church. Tam turned and vowed to his knights, 'Unless they yield these bounds to me, this day some broken heads must be!' He parleyed with his rival, the Abbot of Grange, who stated that Balloch had been granted by King William the Lion to Kinloss Abbey centuries before, but they decide to settle the matter in typical fourteenth-century fashion – a sword duel. Thus continues the ballad penned in 1849 by Banffshire author, John Alexander Cameron, which details the fatal combat between Abbot John and Tam Gordon. Both lose their lives and the Gordons pursue the remaining monks to seek revenge for their kinsman's death.

Tam Gordon was a real laird, born in the early 1400s. Cameron's ballad details Tam's estate as follows:

Daach, Sauchen and Keithock Mill
O' Tam o' Riven owned the will
Balveny, Cults and Clunymore
Auchindroyne an' many more.

He was the son of Elizabeth Cruickshank and Sir John Gordon of Strathbogie who died in 1394, the latter's grandfather having been granted his estate by no less than Robert the Bruce. Tam and his brother John are regarded as the progenitors of the old line of

Gordons in this area. Thus it is no surprise that such a powerful gentleman would take up arms against a local churchman to ensure his borders were not encroached upon. However, it is more likely the 'battle' was administrative rather than involving a display of force. All that remains of this legendary battle are the Monk's Cairn on Balloch Hill, and the effigy of Tam in Ruthven's ruined kirkyard.

Thomas Gordon's descendants went on to build Auchanachie House in 1594, just along the road from Ruthven. The manor stands today, refurbished and clad in traditional sixteenth-century pink render, still a family home. The name Auchanachie, which translates from Gaelic as 'the Merchant's Field', was to become associated with further bloodshed two centuries later, when a brutal murder occurred on the estate at the croft of Upper Auchanachie. The tenant, George Milne, and his daughter were hacked to death by an anonymous axeman who tried to cover up his

crime by razing the house to the ground. Although never proven, the reputed killer was the same Andrew Hosack who ended up on Johnny Milne's gallows in Aberdeen's Castlegate in 1810. This was the reason behind the riot that saw Hosack's corpse end up in the hands of the anatomists, the due punishment for a murderer, despite the fact the court records show Hosack was executed for theft.

3. The Cairnie Murder – Inchtammack Cottage, Drumdelgie Wood

'Twas on December 20th,
The year was 1910,
Then Willie Cummin' killed his wife
In Cairnie's lonely glen.

These are the opening lyrics to the tragic ballad 'The Cairnie Murder', based on a true event which took place in a now demolished cottage near Drumdelgie Wood. On the site stands a modern house erected by the Forestry Commission, with no indication that, over a century ago, this was where William Cumming, a native of Elgin, battered his wife Helen to death with a pair of coal-tongs.

The local press abhorred the vicious, drunken attack by Cumming, attributing the cause to alcohol-fuelled jealousy. Both ballad and newspaper relate how the younger sons, William (eleven) and George (nine) had run barefoot to Huntly to alert the police:

Three miles they ran on muddy road
Withoot a hose or shee,
Wi' nothing but their sarkies on,
Heroic deed tae dee.

Little George, having tried to come between his parents, had sustained numerous head wounds and was covered in both his own and Helen's blood. The local police sergeant quickly heard the boys' statements and raced to Inchtammack Cottage, only to be greeted by the aftermath of the murder. The article in the *Huntly Express* continued:

It only required a cursory glance at the mutilated corpse to acquaint the police officers of what had happened and the cause of death. The spectacle that greeted their gaze was a shocking one, but it was obvious that they could do nothing for the unfortunate woman.

Willie Cumming himself was asleep, perhaps dozing off the booze that had set off this horrible chain of events. The constables woke him up, but he offered no resistance, his bloodstained clothing and his wife's battered body loudly proclaiming his guilt. This was not just an isolated attack: Willie had already assaulted Helen after another drunken spree, which had landed him thirty days in jail. His alcoholism seemed to have sprung from the family's poverty and perhaps the nagging sense that his wife's parents had always disapproved of him.

He would later plead guilty to culpable homicide

at his trial in January 1911 and was sentenced to ten years' imprisonment. The tragedy was soon forgotten by the press, but not by the anonymous balladeer whose words would be sung forty years later to folklorist Hamish Henderson by Turriff housewife Jean Elvin. The ballad was new to Hamish. Jean's husband explained that there was a taboo attached to its performance: 'At one time o' day ye couldnae say that . . . you would get nicked for that.' It would seem that because the murder had occurred within living memory, no one dared to risk upsetting Willie Cumming's descendants. The locals also apparently quashed its performance, determined to shield the Cumming boys from the horrible memory of their mother's untimely end. Even now 'The Cairnie Murder' is seldom sung.

Acknowledgements

Many thanks to: Sebastian and Candida Leslie of Warthill for allowing me to feature their lovely home; Patrick Wight for telling me about 'Auld Dubrach'; David Ryan Keith for agreeing to be interviewed about his film *Redwood Massacre* and supplying a movie still; Alec Westwood for relating Dunnideer's Pagan significance to me; Haworth Hodgkinson for telling me about Byron's connection with Glen Tanar; Alison MacColl for showing me around the kirkyard at Kintore and introducing me to the tragic tale of Trooper Smart; Rev. Robert Thorburn of Fyvie Church for allowing me to photograph his amazing Tiffany window and sharing useful source material concerning its origin; Professor Ian Russell of the Elphinstone Institute, University of Aberdeen, for identifying the site of Inchtammack Cottage where the Cairnie Murder took place; Anthony Robertson, son of Stanley Robertson, the Master Storyteller, for introducing me to 'Auld Craobhie' and sharing more amazing Travellers' tales; Dr Alexander Thain of Inverugie for showing me the castle at the bottom of his garden; the current proprietor of Tonley House for allowing me to photograph the castle ruins; and of course my Mum and Dad for their support in proofing the manuscript and generally supporting me in what is always an exhausting task!

Glossary

Aethling	Aethling is a nickname meaning 'of the royal family'. Applied to Margaret, Queen of Scots, wife of Malcolm III, and her brother, Edgar. The siblings were the great niece and nephew of Edward the Confessor, King of England. Their father was Edward 'the Exile', son of King Edmund 'Ironside' of England. Edgar and Margaret's father died soon after arriving in England with his family. Edgar, as the last of the royal house of Wessex, was in his early teens when his great-uncle Edward died, thus support for him was sparse to say the least. By the time William, Duke of Normandy, was victorious at Hastings, the English were negotiating to make him king, passing over Edgar, due mainly to his youth. Edgar was made a prisoner by William, but then escaped with his family to Scotland, and sanctuary in Malcolm III's court, where the widowed Scots monarch married Margaret in AD 1070.
Alba	Gaelic name for Scotland. From the reign of Kenneth MacAlpin, AD 848, it was the area of Irish Gaelic influence as opposed to the native Pictish peoples of Scotland's East Coast.
Burker	A professional bodysnatcher in the times when recently buried bodies were dug up and stolen to be sold to anatomy schools due to a shortage of cadavers for

educational purposes. Originated with William Burke, one of the Irish navvies charged with the 'West Port Murders' in Edinburgh, c. 1828. Burke was hanged, while his partner in crime, William Hare, escaped by turning King's evidence against him.

Caff sake	Caff or cauff is the Scots word for chaff, as the *Scots Dictionary* defines: 'the outer husks of oats or other cereals, separated from the grain by winnowing, much used as a filling for bedmattresses', hence 'caff sake' was a chaff-filled mattress, 'sake' coming from "sack". Fishermen in Aberdeenshire also used 'caff sakes' in their bunks at sea, as there was a ready supply available from the farms near the coast.
Chiel	Scots word for a boy or young man.
Colonel's Bed	John Farquharson of Inverey's hiding place; a river gorge covered by a wide overhanging rock, on the Ey Burn, Inverey, Braemar. The gorge still exists, but the rock has long since collapsed.
Colophon	According to the OED, 'a statement at the end of a book, typically with a printer's emblem, giving information about its authorship and printing.' In the case of *The Book of Deer*, the scribe was asking for a blessing for himself by all readers of the 'splendid little book'.

Couthy — Scots adjective for someone who is friendly, gregarious and sociable. Can also mean plain or unsophisticated.

Covenanters' Wars — While the Civil War raged in England between the supporters of Oliver Cromwell and Charles I, those in agreement with Cromwell north of the border were the Covenanters, so called because of the 'National Covenant', an agreement drawn up in 1638 in Scotland to reform religion. The basic issue was that Charles had tried to introduce the English service book to the Church of Scotland, which contained forms of worship that were too close to the outlawed Catholicism for the Scots' liking. They wanted to rid the church of bishops and priests and replace it with the Presbyterian form of church government, i.e. a series of courts or 'presbyteries' starting with the lowest, the Kirk Session, rising to the General Assembly. The Scots Covenanters ultimately would hand over the fugitive King Charles to Cromwell. Scots Royalists on the other hand fought bitterly against those of the Covenant party. Although we in Scotland call the conflict 'The Covenanters' Wars', English historians use the phrase 'The War of the Three Kingdoms' making clear the involvement of Scotland, England and Ireland.

Craobhie	Affectionate name for the ancient oak tree favoured by Scottish Travellers as a campsite and meeting place on Lumphanan's old drove road. Based on the Gaelic word 'craobh' meaning tree.
Dowie	Scots adjective meaning 'sad, melancholy, dreary or dull', in use from the mid sixteenth century onwards.
Dubby	Scots adjective for muddy; a 'dub' was a muddy pool of stagnant water.
Earl Marischal	A hereditary office of the Keith family since the twelfth century. The Great Marischal was the monarch's bodyguard at court and custodian of the royal regalia. William Keith was made Earl c. 1458 by James II of Scotland.
Episcopalian	A form of church government involving bishops and priests, used by both the Catholic and Anglican Churches.
Farm Toun	From the Agricultural Revolution onwards, farming developed on a large scale, with enclosed fields and numerous buildings on site, thus in Scotland they were described as 'farm touns' because they literally were a "township" of the workers, the farmer, his family and their livestock. Toun is sometimes spelt 'toon'.
Feel	Scots word for fool.

Fittie	Local name for 'Footdee', planned fishing village built in 1806-09. Fittie is more correct, as it is likely to have come from the Gaelic word for pasture, 'fèithe'.
Fushionless	Lacking in energy or strength when referring to things or people; Scots adjective from the noun 'fushion' meaning energy, life force, etc. In use from the mid nineteenth century.
GNSR	Abbreviation for Great North of Scotland Railway. The Formartine and Buchan line that served most of Aberdeenshire was part of GNSR.
Hurdies	Scots word for buttocks or sometimes hips.
Lord of the Isles	The Gaelic title was Ri Innse Gall, 'King of the Foreign Isles', i.e. the Norse-ruled islands. The first holder of that title was a Scandinavian, Godfrey Haroldson, who was also the accepted progenitor of Clan Donald. The Lordship of the Isles grew out of Godfrey's descendants, most famously, Somerled, a Gall-Gael. Thus all MacDonalds claimed their descent from Somerled. Donald MacDonald, the cousin of Alexander Stewart, who fought at Harlaw, was the 8th Lord of the Isles.
Lucky	Scots nickname for an old woman or grandmother.

Motte-and-bailey	A man-made earth mound surmounted by a keep, usually built of wood, occasionally of stone. Introduced to Britain by the Normans in the eleventh century and was widely adopted by native noblemen and the Norman-French settlers.
Old Pretender	One of the less flattering titles given to James Francis Edward Stuart, son of the deposed James II of Great Britain. James Francis' sister, Mary, and her Dutch Protestant husband, William, were accepted as the new monarchs when their father's open Catholicism terrified the Protestant leaders. Also known as Chevalier St George, and by Jacobites as 'James III', a title that was never his. Father of Charles Edward Stuart, the Young Pretender, Bonnie Prince Charlie.
Pict	Indigenous peoples of Eastern Scotland from the late Iron Age into the Celtic period. They spoke a Brythonic/Welsh tongue described linguistically as P-Celtic, after the main significant sound in the word for 'son', i.e. 'map'.
Pinkie Cleugh, Battle of,	This battle took place in 1547, near Musselburgh, and was the last attempt in a campaign started by Henry VIII to forcibly unite Scotland and England by marrying his heir, Edward VI, to Mary, Queen of Scots. The English army was headed by Edward VI's uncle, Edward Seymour; they comprehensively defeated the Scots using a mixture of modern tactics and the matchless longbow. There were huge casualties on the Scottish side – around 6,000 died.

Ploughgate	Medieval unit of land measurement approximating the land a plough team of eight oxen could till in a single annual season. Also known as an oxgang.
Presbyterian	A form of Christian church government utilising a series of courts from Kirk Session, Presbytery and Synod up to General Assembly. Used by the Protestant Church of Scotland after the Reformation of 1560, which outlawed Catholicism.
River Ugie	Peterhead's main river. It is twenty-nine miles long and has its source in Windyheads, Aberdour. The main tributary is the South Ugie Water.
Smatchet	The *Scots Dictionary* defines this as 'A small insignificant person or animal, freq. applied to a pert or mischievous child, a little rogue', and occasionally when applied to an adult, 'an impudent worthless character'. This is what Peter Grant, Auld Dubrach, would have meant when insulting the government troops at Culloden.
Thomas the Rhymer	Also known as Thomas Learmonth of Erceldoune. A noted seer and prophet of the thirteenth century, celebrated in the ballad 'Thomas the Rhymer'. Had a habit of cursing anyone who did not pay him sufficient respect.
Torry Battery	A former artillery battery first manned by Aberdeen's volunteer militia from the 1860s. It was used in both world wars for defence; Beaufort guns were stationed there.

Bibliography

Adams, Norman, *Hangman's Brae, North East Scotland's Lawbreakers and Law Enforcers* (Edinburgh: Black & White, 2005).

Anon., *Directory to noblemen and gentlemen's seats, villages etc, in Scotland* (Edinburgh: Sutherland & Knox, 1857).

Anon., *The Scottish Journal of Topography, Antiquities and Traditions*, vol. 1, Sep. 1847 – Feb. 1848 (Edinburgh: Thomas George Stevenson, 1848).

Berresford Ellis, Peter, Macbeth: *High King of Scotland, 1040-1057 AD* (London: Frederick Muller Ltd, 1980).

Bertie, David M. (ed.), *Scottish Episcopal Clergy 1689-2000* (London: T&T Clark, 2000).

Campbell, Duncan B., *Mons Graupius AD 83: Rome's Battle at the Edge of the World* (Oxford: Osprey, 2010).

Cope, Julian, *The Modern Antiquarian: A Pre-Millennial Odyssey through Megalithic Britain* (London: Harper Collins/ Thorsons, Reissue, 2011).

Fouin, François Louis Pierre, *Glen Tanar: Valley of Echoes and Hidden Treasures* (Inverurie, Aberdeenshire: Leopard Press/ Fouin Books, 2009).

Gill, Andrew John Mitchell, *The Families of Moir and Byres* (Edinburgh & Aberdeen: Scott & Ferguson and D. Wyllie & Son, 1885).

MacDonald, James, *Place Names in Strathbogie, with notes historical, antiquarian and descriptive* (Aberdeen: D. Wyllie & Son, 1891).

MacLeod, Nicholas Kenneth, *The Churches of Buchan and Notes by the Way* (Aberdeen/Edinburgh: A&R Milne and John Menzies & Co., 1899).

McConnochie, Alex Inkson, *Donside*, Aberdeenshire Classics (Aberdeen: James G. Bisset, 1985).

McConnochie, Alex Inkson, *Deeside*, Aberdeenshire Classics (Aberdeen: James G. Bisset, 1985).

Milne, John, *Celtic Place-Names in Aberdeenshire* (Aberdeen: Aberdeen Daily Journal for the Carnegie Trust, 1912).

Moore, Thomas, *Life of Lord Byron (With His Letters and Journals)*, Vols I-V (1835).

Murray, Ian, *The Dee from the Far Cairngorms: Folklore and History from the Glens of Royal Deeside* (Ballater, Aberdeenshire: Lochnagar Publishing, 1999).

Paterson, Raymond Campbell, *The Lords of the Isles: a History of Clan Donald* (Edinburgh: Birlinn, 2001; reprint 2008).

Pratt, John B., *Buchan* (London: L. Smith & Son, 1901).

Pratt, John B., *The Life and Death of Jamie Fleeman, the Laird of Udny's Fool* (Aberdeen: Lewis & James Smith, 1859).

Royal Society of Edinburgh, *First Report by the Committee on Boulders appointed by the Royal Society of Edinburgh in 1871* (Edinburgh: Neill & Co., 1872).

Scott, Hew, *Fasti Ecclesiae Scoticanae: The Succession of Ministers in the Church of Scotland from the Reformation, Vol. VI, Synods of Aberdeen and of Moray* (Edinburgh, Scotland: Oliver & Boyd, New Edition, 1926).